Five Minutes A Day Dream-Action Path
Dream the Life & World You Desire, Then Create It!

Praise for Jan Gault's New Book . . .

"A key premise is that the world's fate lies in the hands of individual citizens, and that each of us can make those choices in our day-to-day affairs that will move us toward a better world for our children and grandchildren. Along with a seven step process for personal-global change, Jan gives you dozens of specific actions you can take in your spare time to create a more compassionate and just world."
~**Arun Gandhi**
Former President
M.K. Gandhi Institute for Nonviolence
http://www.gandhiinstitute.net

"This book is for spiritual revolutionaries and evolutionary change agents. It is based on a deep understanding of the psychospiritual dimensions of transformation. It is time to integrate the frontiers of psychology and mind science into practices that will propagate love and wisdom. Jan Gault has given us an excellent roadmap."
~**James O'Dea**
Former President
Institute of Noetic Sciences
http://www.noetic.org

"A refreshing and encouraging piece that offers concrete steps to help each individual find their own unique way to 'change the world.' A gentle, but powerful, wake-up call to action. Should be required Social Studies reading for all students growing up in today's world."
~**Connie Mitchell**
Executive Director, Institute of Human Services
http://www.ihshawaii.org

"This book provides an antidote to the apathy that can often come from feeling overwhelmed by one's role in shaping the future of society and the planet. The capacity to make a difference comes from tapping into one's own inner strengths and learning how to act on one's values in the community. This practical book simplifies the process so that people can make effective choices to serve themselves and the world around them."
**~Michael Kramer
Managing Partner, Natural Investments LLC**
http://www.naturalinvesting.com

"When our hope is to create a more compassionate and just world, it's easy to feel daunted by the sheer enormity of the task, or to give up because we don't know where to begin. Jan shows us that we don't have to obliterate our personal dreams and goals to become good global citizens. Jan suggests dozens of specific actions you can take in your spare time to turn your idealism into reality, while the beliefs that sustain your global involvement energize your personal dreams as well."
**~Madeleine Van Hecke, Ph.D.
Author of *Blind Spots:
Why Smart People Do Dumb Things***
www.overcomeblindspots.com

"This book provides a great incentive to do good things for our world and to truly motivate us to make the world a better place for all. It should be inspirational reading for us all, no matter where we live, who we are, or whatever our circumstances. I would recommend this book as a major resource for all civic organizations."
**~Rev. Sam Cox
Treasurer, Interfaith Alliance Hawaii**
http://www.interfaithalliancehawaii.org

"This is a practical, 'can-do' primer that challenges and empowers each of us to look beyond our own day-to-day routines and become a global citizen. Thought-provoking questions and meaningful activities allow the reader to methodically explore the best way to take responsibility in changing our precious world. This is a very worthwhile read."
~**Lester Stiefel**
Senior Vice President, Human Resources
Bank of Hawaii

"So often we think, as individuals, we cannot make a difference—that only extraordinary and powerful people make meaningful contributions. This book shows how, indeed, as ordinary individuals, there is a lot we can do. So why wait? Take the first step now!"
~**Patricia Ellis**
Executive Director
Hawaii Center For Attitudinal Healing
www.attitudinalhealinghawaii.org

"Dr. Jan details qualities of the emerging global person who thinks and acts within the context of an interdependent world. Author Jan Gault's position is that, as more of us take personal responsibility for the state of the world, and educate ourselves in simple, everyday, socially responsible choices, the world will change for the better—and so will we! Definitely a worthwhile read!"
~**Dr. Saleem Ahmed**
Founder, All Believers Network
Author: *Islam: A Religion of Peace?*
www.IslamAReligionOfPeace.com

"An antidote to global-crisis-overwhelm, Jan Gault gives us practical and sound advice for taking personal action on world issues. Remember, you may only be one person, but there are six billion of you out there!"
~**Christine Butler**
Editor, *Action Change* e-Magazine
www.actionchange.com

"In simple, concrete messages, Jan Gault tells all of us how to be peaceful, interdependent citizens of this global community. Indeed, Teaching Tolerance begins with the Self and spreads outward to all other beings."
~**Jeff Sapp**
Senior Curriculum Specialist/Writer
Teaching Tolerance Magazine
www.teachingtolerance.org

"Are you feeling overwhelmed by the news today? Here is a book that brings inspiration and hope, giving you the resources to be the global citizen that you aspire to be."
~**Kirsten Moller**
Executive Director, Global Exchange
http://www.globalexchange.org

"At long last, I finally was able to sit down and enjoy your entire book, and what a wonderful book it is! You've provided a systematic approach to changing some of the toughest, most resistant things we have . . . our beliefs. And, you've done it with grace, humor, and grounded optimism that befits your years of experience. You've provided a real service in writing this book and it deserves a wide audience. Indeed, the world deserves your book to have a wide audience!"
~Alan Zulch
Director of Networking, Global MindShift
http://www.global-mindshift.org

"This book will open your divine heart toward a new healthy and happy life. It is a wisdom of the soul. . . . It is time for self-realization. Do it now."
~Yogi Ramesh
President/CEO, Universal Yoga
www.universalyoga.org

*"**5 Minutes A Day Dream-Action Path** is a terrific guide to creating an intentional, meaningful life of global citizenry."*
~Linda Stuart
Executive Director, Global Citizens Network
http://www.globalcitizens.org

Five Minutes A Day Dream-Action Path

Dream the Life & World You Desire Then Create It!

Also by Jan Gault

BOOKS
Motivational Messages for Miracle Moments
Quotes, Questions & Actions for Global Understanding
The Mighty Power of Your Beliefs
Play Your Way to Prosperity
Free Time: Making Your Leisure Count

AUDIO/CD PROGRAMS
Inspirational/Motivational Podcasts
Perseverance & Passion: Strategies for Success
25 Ways to Build Self-Esteem & Success
The Principle of Purpose
Vision & Courage
Prosperity Principles & Beliefs

PERSONAL-GLOBAL EMPOWERMENT & PROSPERITY SERIES
Explorations & Inspirational Messages
7 Steps to Personal-Global Empowerment
Personal-Global Empowerment Calendar
Choices for a Better Life, Community & World

Books are available at quantity discounts with bulk purchase for business, educational, or sales promotional use. For information, please telephone 415-367-3513 or Email **prosper@drjan.net.**

For information on scheduling Jan to speak at your next event, or on ordering books, CDs, and other products by Jan, please Email info@drjan.net or visit www.drjan.net.

Online Audio/Video Consultations with Dr. Jan Are Currently Available

Five Minutes A Day Dream-Action Path

Dream the Life & World You Desire Then Create It!

Jan L. Gault, Ph.D.
http://www.drjan.net

Ocean Manor

Cover Design by Robert Howard, Bookgraphics
Book interior layout by MacGraphics Services
Indexing by Clive Pyne Book Indexing Services

© 2009 by Jan L. Gault

All rights reserved, including the right of reproduction in whole or in part in any form.

Requests for permission or further information should be addressed to

Ocean Manor, P.O. Box 2701, Kailua-Kona, Hawaii 96745.

Publishers Cataloging in Publication Data

Gault, Jan L.
    Five minutes a day dream-action path : dream the life & world you desire then create it! / Jan L. Gault. -- 1st ed. -- c2009.
       p. ; cm.
    ISBN: 978-0-923699-90-1 (pbk.)
    Includes bibliographical references and index.

       1. Self-help techniques. 2. Self-actualization (Psychology)
    3. Achievement motivation. 4. Success--Psychological aspects.
      I. Title. II. Title: Five minutes a day dream action path.
BF632 .G38 2009   2009904078
158/.1--dc22   0908

    Library of Congress Control Number: 2009904078

Manufactured in the United States of America
10 9 8 7 6 5 4 3 2 1

This book is printed on acid-free paper.

Disclaimer

Neither author Jan Gault nor the publisher assumes responsibility or liability arising from the use of any information contained in this book. Under no circumstances shall Jan Gault, Jan Gault International, or Ocean Manor Publishing be liable for any direct, indirect, punitive, incidental, special, or consequential damages arising out of or in any way connectedwith the use of *Five Minutes A Day Dream-Action Path*.

This book is dedicated to all the caring, courageous, and compassionate women and men striving to tilt the balance of prosperity and peace to people everywhere. I also dedicate it to all the wonderful people acting to make a difference within my

Favorite Causes and Organizations

Action Without Borders, Alliance Network, Amnesty International, Audubon Society, Better World Club, Books for a Better World, Center for Global Nonviolence, Citizens for Global Solutions, Childreach, Common Cause, Doctors Without Borders, Educators for Social Responsibility, Feminist Majority Foundation, M. K. Gandhi Institute for Nonviolence, Global Citizens Network, Global Exchange, Global Heroes, Global MindShift, The Group of 1000, Habitat for Humanity, Human Rights Education Associates, Human Rights Watch, International Federation of University Women, Institute of Noetic Sciences, Interfaith Alliance, Katalysis, Kiva, Modest Needs, Nature Conservatory, Ocean Conservatory, Oxfam International, Peace X Peace, Practical Action, Psychologists for Social Responsibility, Red Hat Society, Seva Foundation, Sierra Club, Society for the Psychological Study of Social Issues, Soroptimist International, Southern Poverty Law Center, St. Labre Indian School, Universal Flag, White Ribbon Campaign, Worldwatch Institute, Women's International Center, Women for Women International

Contents

Acknowledgments	xix
Preface	1
Global Challenges: Did You Know?	3

I
LAYING THE GROUNDWORK
PERSONAL-GLOBAL CHANGE DYNAMICS

Chapter 1	Global Citizens Are Changing the World!	11
Chapter 2	Change Begins With You!	15
Chapter 3	Belief-Energy-Action Dynamics	23

II
GET STARTED AND GET EXCITED
CREATE YOUR PERSONAL-GLOBAL VISION

Steps 1, 2, 3

Chapter 4	Dream the Life & World You Desire!	31
Chapter 5	Target Areas for Change	37
Chapter 6	Map Out Your Personal-Global Dreams	43

III
CHALLENGES TO CHANGE
BREAK FREE FROM BELIEF BARRIERS FOILING YOUR DREAMS

Step 4

Chapter 7	Banish Belief Barriers Preventing Effective Action	53
Chapter 8	Stamp Out Beliefs That Are Limiting Prosperity	63
Chapter 9	Eject Beliefs Harmful to Better Communication and Understanding	77
Chapter 10	Purge Toxic Beliefs That Impede Educational Ideals	83

IV
CHARGE UP BELIEFS AND
MIND BOOSTERS TO POWER YOUR DREAMS

Chapter 11	Build a Belief Bank That Empowers Your Life and World	93
Chapter 12	Give Yourself an Edge With Belief Boosters!	103
Chapter 13	Expand Your Horizons With High-Impact Questions	109

V
PUT YOUR DREAMS INTO ACTION!
ACTIONS FOR A BETTER LIFE AND WORLD

Step 5

Chapter 14	Develop Mental-Action Habits to Reinforce Your Vision	115
Chapter 15	Take Action for Personal-Global Prosperity	119
Chapter 16	Act to Build Better Communication and Understanding	127
Chapter 17	Actions for a Sounder and Saner Education	133

VI
STAYING MOTIVATED
KEEPING THE MOMENTUM ALIVE

Step 6

Chapter 18	Design Your Time Plan: Set Target Dates and Track Your Progress	141
Chapter 19	Five Minutes a Day Is All It Takes!	151

VII
CONGRATULATE YOURSELF AND CELEBRATE!

Step 7

Chapter 20	Congratulate Yourself and Reap the Rewards!	157

VIII
Epilogue

The Mind-Heart Distinction 163

IX
Resource Directory

Choices for a Better Life, Community, and World 171
Quotations to Motivate and Prompt Action 173
More Actions for a Better Life and World 175
Three Actions You Are Taking for Personal-Global Empowerment and Prosperity 211
Global Citizen Pledge 212
Bibliography: Books Making A Global Difference 213

X
Appendix

List of Activities 223
Notes 227
Index 235
Author Profile 247

Acknowledgments

Accolades to all the fine organizations, groups, and dedicated individuals working to bring a better world into being. Your efforts and your commitment to positive world change continue to strengthen my own resolve and purpose.

I feel truly blessed and am thankful for the many authors who have written books to inspire, motivate, and bring hope to people everywhere. I'm especially grateful for the books by Gregg Braden, Jack Canfield, Deepak Chopra, Alan Cohen, Andrew Cohen, Dr. Wayne Dyer, Riane Eisler, Marilyn Ferguson, Arun Gandhi, Guy Finley, Mark Hansen, Dr. Willis Harman, Louise Hay, Hazel Henderson, Jean Houston, Barbara Marx Hubbard, Ervin Laszlo, Bruce Lipton, Robert Quinn, Michael Nagler, James Ray, Bernie Seigel, Joe Vitale, Ken Wilbur, Muhammad Yunus, and oh so many more. My heartfelt thanks to each of you for your writings and work!

I have also learned immeasurably from the universities where I've taught classes in Life Span Development, Psychology of Personality, Social Psychology, and Guidance and Counseling. I especially want to thank the administration, faculty, and students at the University of

Hawaii, Hawaii Pacific University, University of Phoenix, and Central Texas College, who have enriched my understanding in countless ways.

I am deeply grateful to the kind and generous individuals listed in the front pages who took time out of their busy schedules to read this book, provide feedback, and write the thoughtful testimonials.

A big mahalo to all my Hawaii friends, my clients, and students worldwide who filled out my questionnaire for this book, and provided me with comments and suggestions.

I especially am indebted to my publicist, Catherine Graham, for her many hours contacting individuals, organizations, and media. Her friendship and her belief in my work have been great sources of pleasure.

Thanks also to . . .

- William Prescott, for his encouragement and insightful comments on the book. His thoughtful and helpful reflections and recommendations have definitely added to the value of this work.

- John Kremer, marketing authority, for his many valuable suggestions on the cover text and design.

- My copy editor, Kathy K. Grow, for her professionalism, thoroughness, and positive attitude. She has met all my expectations for what an editor should be. It was a pleasure working with her.

- My indexer, Clive Pyne, for the amazing job he did in pulling together all the book's data. He has been a delight to work with.

- Karen Saunders and Lindsey Hurwitz, my interior designers, for their patience, helpfulness and fine work.

I greatly appreciate my volunteers, Jennifer Thorne, Melissa McCrory, Neal Jensen, and Nylea Lace, who offered their time so generously, and provided me with the extra hours I needed to complete this book.

Others I want to mention are my fitness trainers, my yoga instructors, and my NIA dance instructors, all of whom helped keep me in shape physically, and energized to meet the demands of my work.

I also want to thank my Social Media Friends, particularly Twitter and Facebook friends, for their inspiring message postings, and fun breaks online that made my writing experience go more enjoyably.

I am grateful to all who have signed the Global Citizen Pledge and the growing body of world citizens living lifestyles that promote prosperity and positive global change.

I am appreciative of the musicians and artists whose beautiful music, artwork, and film have inspired and uplifted my soul—keeping me on track whenever I was inclined to feel otherwise. I've been encouraged by Spiritual Cinema Circle's inspiring, positive movies and documentaries, enriching so many lives and serving to offset the impact of negative media messages. Also especially close to my heart is the rhythmic Hawaiian music that reaches deep within my soul, reminding me always of life's great song and meaning.

I would be remiss if I did not also acknowledge the Universal Energy that flows through life and keeps me on the path of my purpose. I appreciate the miracle of nature's wonders, especially the soothing ocean waves and swaying palm trees outside my window that thrilled and delighted me daily as I sat at my computer to complete this book.

Finally, I take full responsibility for any mistakes, omissions, and errors in this work.

Preface

Let us choose "to believe something good can happen.
~J. Martin Kohe"

The pages ahead are not a protest about what's wrong with the world, but a celebration of what's right, and what each of us can do in our discretionary time to have a positive global impact.

The vast majority of humans are kind, compassionate, thoughtful, and generous people. In researching this book, I was both surprised and encouraged when I learned how many dedicated individuals and organizations are working toward a better world. Literally thousands of organizations and countless individuals from all walks of life are involved directly or indirectly in ending widespread social and economic injustices, helping families in war-torn countries put their lives back together, and improving educational opportunities. These are not just those you might think of as activists and advocates, but housewives, teachers, students, writers, scientists, artists, and people from virtually every walk of life.

Nonetheless, many of us would like to learn how to do more to improve the world situation. As a social psychologist, I felt I could perhaps offer a unique perspective that would be helpful toward this end.

I was first inspired by Mark Harris in an article he wrote for *Conscious Choice Magazine* suggesting it was a shame most psychologists had such a myopic view and didn't add their voices and expertise to pressing world issues. His statement struck home for me. Guilty as charged! My consultations, writings, and books have mostly focused on individual empowerment and prosperity. I needed a broader vision that embraced both individual and global well-being.

After much research and reflection, the pages of this book began to take shape. And I learned a delightful truth! When we act in the service of all humanity, we ourselves become healthier and happier. Making choices within the context of all people, changes the world for the better *and* puts more meaning into our own lives. Better yet, it's something we can do in our spare time! What a happy revelation! In the pages that follow, you will learn how only five minutes a day can improve the world *and* transform your own life.

Other than giving you a brief overview of some of the challenges facing the world today, my purpose is not to talk about what's wrong, but to build on our strengths and what we're doing right so we can keep a vision of possibilities and positive outcomes. With this vision, we are positioned to move forward, taking specific actions to make a difference in our lives at home and around the globe.

Global Challenges: Did You Know?

> *Man uses his intelligence less in the care of his own species than he does in his care of anything else he owns or governs.*
> *~Abraham Meyerson*

Poverty:
- Women and children account for over 70 percent of the 1.2 billion persons living in desperate poverty.[1]

Education:
- More than half the adult population in twenty-three countries is illiterate.[2]
- Women comprise two-thirds of the world's 876 million illiterates.[3]

Work/Inequality:
- Women make up only one-third of the world's labor force, except in northern Africa and western Asia, where the number is much smaller.[4]
- Of the roughly six billion people in the world today, four billion are classified by the World Bank as living in "low income" or "lower middle income" countries. Nearly three billion (2.8) live on less than $2 per day, and 1.2 billion live on less than $1 a day. The vast majority of those living in abject poverty are women.[5]
- Income distribution in the United States is the most inequitable of all the advanced democracies, with 27 percent of blacks and 30 percent of Hispanics in the United States living below the poverty line. On

some Indian reservations in the United States, the unemployment rate is over 70 percent.[6]
- Inequality has increased in many countries, despite positive income growth.[7]

Health:
- More than one billion people lack access to safe drinking water.[8]
- A child dies every fifteen seconds from water-related diseases.[9]
- Globally, women account for half of all cases of HIV/AIDS. In countries with high HIV rates, young women have a higher risk of contracting AIDS than do young men.[10]
- An African woman's lifetime risk of dying from pregnancy-related causes is 1 in 16; in Asia, 1 in 65; and in Europe, 1 in 1,400.[11]
- Children under age five die at rates of more than one in ten in over thirty-five countries.[12]
- Each year, seventeen million people die of diseases that we know how to cure.[13]

Human Rights Violations:
- Millions of girls and women worldwide are physically and sexually abused.[14]
- Over twelve million people worldwide are trafficked into forced labor, the sex trade, and child labor.[15]
- More than half of all women and girls in some African countries have been subjected to female genital mutilation.[16]
- Women and girls comprise more than half the world's refugees, and, as such, have been particularly vulnerable to sexual violence in refugee camps and during flight and resettlement.[17]
- Rape of women during war is intentionally used by many governments as a weapon.[18,19]

- One of every three women—nearly one billion—are beaten, coerced into sex, or otherwise abused in their lifetimes.[20]
- While over ninety-two nations have banned the death penalty, several nations (including China, Iran, Saudi Arabia, and the United States) continue with this barbaric practice, in spite of overwhelming evidence that it does nothing to deter crime. And the appeal process costs taxpayers in the United States more money than life imprisonment.[21]

Political Decision Making:
- Throughout the world, women continue to be significantly underrepresented in political parties, governments, and the United Nations.[22]

Nature and Environment:
- One global conservation organization reports that humans have destroyed more than 30 percent of the natural world since 1970.[23]
- There is overwhelming scientific consensus that the climate is changing, the earth is warming up, and climate change may be one of the greatest threats facing our planet.[24]

The Dilemma of Today's World

We are so inundated by the media with cases of suffering, poverty, and mass starvation in the world today, our minds have difficulty responding. Though our hearts are moved, and we yearn to take some action that will truly make a difference, mostly we feel at a loss about what to do. The issues are complex, the problems seemingly insurmountable: can any one individual have an impact? I believe the answer to this question is a loud and resounding YES!

Nor do you need to be an extraordinary individual or an activist. Each of us in our own way and according to our special circumstances has a role to play as a change agent. It's a role that needn't infringe on your other commitments, values, or time constraints, and a role that expands, enhances, and energizes your personal growth and prosperity.

We'll begin our excursion toward a better life and world by examining the characteristics of the emerging global person. Next, you'll learn how to make your spare time count by taking seven interactive steps toward personal-global empowerment and prosperity. By following the steps outlined, you'll not only be impacting world change but reaping the joyous rewards of personal fulfillment.

Part I

LAYING THE GROUNDWORK
PERSONAL-GLOBAL CHANGE DYNAMICS

> *Optimism is a strategy for making a better future. Because unless you believe that the future can be better, it's unlikely you will step up and take responsibility for making it so. If you assume that there's no hope, you guarantee that there will be no hope. If you assume that there is an instinct for freedom, there are opportunities to change things, there's a chance you may contribute to making a better world.*
> *The choice is yours.*
> ~Noam Chomsky

Chapter One

Global Citizens Are Changing the World!

We should not say "I am an Athenian" or "I am a Roman" but "I am a Citizen of the Universe."
-Marcus Aurelius

Becoming a Global Citizen

Today we see global persons emerging in virtually every country. These are people who know no boundaries, and, instead of holding an individualistic worldview that puts me, mine, and my country first, are attuned to the needs and desires of all humanity, staying abreast of world events, and living in ways that promote the best interests of people everywhere.

We live in an interdependent world in which our decisions and actions at home impact lives around the globe. Through our collective choices and actions, a child in a war-torn country may have access to clean water to drink and opportunities to attend school—or may not. An innocent woman in Iran may be stoned to death or set free. The dollars we spend as a consumer and investor can enhance or harm the quality of life for those less fortunate. In turn, our own prosperity and well-being are dependent on embracing a larger vision and responsibility.

> *We are not going to be able to operate our Spaceship Earth successfully nor for much longer unless we see it as a whole spaceship and our fate as common. It has to be everybody or nobody.*
> *~Buckminster Fuller*

How does a global citizen think, feel, and act?

- A global person is proactive, and informed about the many ways in which his daily activities make a difference in lives around the world.

- A global person starts with herself, knowing that only by taking care of her own mental, emotional, spiritual, and physical health can she be an effective agent of change. Only then can she set a good example for others.

- A global person knows that by staying healthy, confident, and spiritually clear, she will be less self-absorbed and more able to seek ways to meet the needs of those less fortunate. This in turn enriches her own well-being.

- A global person is motivated to serve his community in ways that benefit all.

- A global person appreciates and learns from differences. She is nonjudgmental and accepting, looking for the best in others and for common cultural bonds. Ideological differences and practices are approached with an open mind, and with a view toward educating and influencing others through nonviolent means whenever a culture's abusive tactics or social injustices are deemed harmful to the human family.

- A global person strives to free her thinking from the misconceptions of past conditioning, and not fall prey to faulty mind-traps such as either-or thinking: I'm right and you're wrong . . . my country, right or wrong. She recognizes that there are more than two sides to most disagreements, and looks for more encompassing visions in which neither person nor nation has to be wrong. A global person searches for common ground and possibilities for cooperation.

- A global person holds a sustainable vision of world prosperity, universal education, socioeconomic justice, and peace.

> *What you hold in your thoughts is what you bring into the world.*
> *– High Star*

In other words, whatever his cultural background, ethnic group, race, gender, or national heritage may be, a global citizen acts out of a worldview that considers the best interests of all humanity.

As global citizens, our personal desires and dreams of prosperity reach out across the oceans, across boundaries, to engulf the well-being of all people and nations. Acting in ways that support the good of each person, rekindles our own energy and the spirit of global peace.

What specifically can a global person do to make a difference?

Listed below are just a few of the actions being taken by global citizens, now making a difference in their lives and around the world:

- Establishing a friendship link with a woman in another culture begins to build understanding and cross-cultural trust.

- A loan to a micro-lender in a Third World country assists a person to start a business enterprise and help her local community reduce poverty. An amount as small as $10 can make a difference between abject poverty and survival for a mother and her baby!

- Taking a vacation to another country and volunteering your time for one to three weeks at a local orphanage builds cultural goodwill and better relationships.

- Making airline travel arrangements through a socially responsible travel agent that puts carbon dioxide emitted by the airline back into the atmosphere, helps reduce the harmful effects of global warming.

- A small monthly donation helps a woman in a war-torn country by giving her the skills to help herself and become an independent, productive citizen.

- Switching to a credit card set up so a portion of your expenditures go to a humanitarian organization such as Amnesty International, helps free innocent victims.

- Deciding to walk or to ride a bike more often keeps you healthier, while lessening traffic congestion and smog.

Our everyday choices make a difference in more ways than most of us can ever begin to imagine. In a later section of this book, you'll be given more than sixty specific actions from which to choose, all of which can help you make a difference. Many of these require less than a minute of your time.

> *Great opportunities to help others seldom come,*
> *but small ones surround us daily.*
> ~Sally Koch

Chapter Two

Change Begins With You!

"They must often change, who would be constant in happiness or wisdom."
~ Confucius

A Cognitive-Action Program for Change

In the chapters that follow, you will progress through seven interactive steps for creating positive change in your life and in the world. The social-psychological principles used to improve individual lives can also be applied on a larger scale for positive cultural change and global understanding. The dynamics and lessons of positive change are constant whether at a micro (individual) or macro (societal) level. You are about to embark on an adventure designed to tap into your unique personality, spark your passion, and move you, me, and all of us toward a brighter future.

The Change Process: You Make the Difference!

> *If you want the Earth to become a planet of peace,*
> *you must become a person of peace.*
> *~ Gary Zukov*

Global change begins with the individual. Mohandas Gandhi wrote: "We must be the change we wish to see in the world." You are a microcosm of the world. When we learn to consistently apply compassion, kindness, and respect to those around us, everyone benefits. When you better understand how your mind's content—your beliefs, thoughts, and emotions—function, you become more adept at improving your personal life, realizing your goals, and, in the process, positioning yourself for helping others.

Achieving your personal desires and dreams is fully compatible with living a lifestyle that supports positive global change. Nor do you need to take on any additional responsibilities or obligations. When you integrate your personal goals with a global mission, you will actually find that you have *more* time and energy for yourself, family, and local community.

The idea is to make a mental shift in your perspective and vision so that they embrace the whole human family. Although the distances between individuals and nations can span thousands of miles, we are all interconnected and affected by one another's respective beliefs and practices. A change in one corner of the world reverberates throughout the international community, touching every person's life, impacting our family's and our community's welfare. Our personal prosperity and well-being are contingent on the healthy dynamics of all humanity and nature.

As we learn to view the world through global eyes, our compassion and vision expand to contain the welfare of all humanity. Our heart connects with the trials and triumphs of each human soul, dissolving adversarial differences that breed anger and revenge.

A Threefold Purpose

My purpose for you is threefold:

First, to provide *a deeper awareness* of some of the issues that affect us all, no matter where we live, or what our occupation, religion, political affiliation, or socioeconomic status might be. By expanding our global perspective and awareness, we expand our power to influence positively the course of events, individually and collectively.

Second, to give you *a personal change program that embodies positive global change.* The scope of this book targets your discretionary time, or time after work.

And, third, to offer you *specific actions that you can start taking immediately to make a difference in your life and the world.*

A Cognitive-Action Paradigm

The interactive cognitive-action paradigm I'll be discussing is basically very simple. Your beliefs, thoughts, and thinking habits trigger your emotions and feelings. Together, these determine your choices and actions. In other words, there is a direct link between your personal beliefs and your experiences, or the quality of your life.

Cognitive-Action Paradigm

For most of us, there is a gap between where we are and where we'd like to be—successful, prosperous, happy, and feeling we've given our best shot during our brief stay on earth.

This gap between where you are now (actual reality) and where you'd like to be (ideal reality) is made up of your beliefs and thoughts. The more limiting the beliefs you have, the greater the gap between where you are now and where you'd like to be, i.e., living your hopes and dreams.

The same principle applies on a larger scale. The gap between where we are now (actual world situation) and where we'd like to be (ideal world situation) is a function of our collective limiting, dysfunctional beliefs. And the more limiting, dysfunctional beliefs we as a world community have, the farther removed we are from a world that encompasses open communication, cooperation, and understanding. The greater our sum total of destructive and detrimental beliefs, the more prone we are to all those things we do not want: suspicion, distrust, poverty, violence, social injustice, and economic inequities.

Many of the beliefs we hold today are compromising humanity's health, imperiling our personal-global welfare, and threatening our survival. A global predominance of faulty beliefs distances us from positive goals, results in lack of intercultural cooperation, and generates disharmony.

Basic Tenets for Socially Responsible Change

The basic tenets necessary for permanent and ongoing socially responsible change to occur, whether at an individual or global level, include the following:

- *Change is wrought through educational means and influence.* We need solid information based on facts—not myths—and instruction in social-psychological tools of learning.

- ***Change begins with the content of the mind, in particular our beliefs and thinking habits.*** We can only think with the information we have stored in our heads. If the content of our mind is clouded with erroneous beliefs and misconceptions about human nature, the universe, different cultures, poverty and prosperity, ethnic groups, gender, environment, health, happiness, and power—to mention but a few—this will be reflected in our decisions and daily activities.

    Especially important are the beliefs we hold about ourselves, i.e., our self-concept, our identity, and our beliefs about others and the universe. Examining our beliefs, thinking habits, and the ways in which they trigger our emotional responses, paves the way for more enlightened choices and actions. Sound beliefs result in sound choices and practices. Unsound beliefs result in unsound choices and practices.

- ***Focus is on the present.*** That is, our focus must be on the present mental-emotional state of the individual and current world community—*not* the past history of a person or the world. The past does not necessarily equal the future—IF we start doing things differently. Just because you have been unable to achieve the level of success and prosperity you desire, does not mean that you cannot improve your future situation. Just because we have always had world poverty and hunger for a huge portion of the world's population, doesn't mean it must continue in the future.

    Just because we continue to have domestic violence and unhealthy conflicts among individuals, doesn't mean they need to continue. And just because armed conflicts and wars are prevalent in the world today, doesn't mean they cannot end. Given motivation, correct information, and viable mental tools, positive individual and global change is a ***real possibility.***

I want you to get excited about this! It is within your means to move the world in powerful new directions! Riane Eisler in *The Chalice and the Blade* reminds us,

" ... [W]hat we think of as natural and inevitable ... domestic violence, chronic warfare, racial and religious prejudice, and the domination of women by men, are not natural or inevitable at all."[1]

- *Personal goals and world community goals must be specific and measurable—not fuzzy, ambiguous concepts.* This ensures that we stay on the right path, learning what works and what doesn't. It means using the scientific method of careful observation, collecting factual information, developing hypotheses, testing them out in experience, and making modifications according to the results. Using precision in our thinking and goals is fully compatible with raising our collective spiritual consciousness. Science and the art of enlightened thinking go hand-in-hand.

- *The approach you'll learn is results-oriented, maintaining a constant and positively charged vision of the desired outcomes.* Emphasis is placed on what people and cultures are doing right, not wrong. Our vision is one of possibilities and solutions over problems. Responsible change builds on strengths, rather than weaknesses. What you focus on expands. We need to keep our vision on ideal outcomes, not potential problems.

    For example, instead of being *against* poverty, suffering, and social injustices, our focus is on maintaining a world vision of affluence, in which every person's basic needs for food, shelter, and clothing are met, and a world of caring, compassionate global citizens, who exemplify the principles of social and economic justice.

Personal Beliefs Are Linked to the Quality of Life

To reiterate, there is a direct link between your personal beliefs and the quality of your life. And there is a direct link between our collective personal beliefs and the quality of life for humanity. The net effect is the world as we see it today. To generate positive change, we need to build our mental storehouse of empowering beliefs and then implement them in action.

Stated simply, change involves targeting an area for change, identifying any limiting beliefs held in that area, displacing them with empowering beliefs, and reinforcing each in action.

Globally, this means identifying those collective destructive beliefs that are widening the gap between a world of poverty, scarcity, and suffering (current world situation), and a world of prosperity, cooperation, and understanding (ideal world vision). Only by displacing the old limiting beliefs with universal empowering beliefs that result in effective action strategies, can we move toward a world we can all feel good, and not guilty, about.

This is neither a utopian pipe dream nor a bid for cultural conformity. Cultural diversity can best be preserved around the world through gaining a better understanding of human nature, belief-energy dynamics, and the common denominators of decision making, leading to behavior.

Whether a person is living in Africa, Afghanistan, or America, the social-psychological dynamics of change are the same. The more we do to educate each person on the face of the earth about how her mind works—how our mental makeup of beliefs, perceptions, and styles of thinking elicit our emotions, choices, and actions—the greater our hope for a truly civilized world.

Having a head filled with hazy half-truths and cultural misconceptions that we've picked up unwittingly from childhood experiences and mainstream media, can only result in unwise choices and detrimental actions. A natural tendency is to believe that we are right and superior, and it's *they* who are wrong. Yet, we all have much to learn from each other, and improve those thinking habits that thwart intercultural cooperation and understanding.

The idea is to shift our thinking away from judgments about which beliefs are morally right or wrong, superior or inferior, and to seek areas of commonality in which we can learn and grow together as a human family in wisdom, kindness, and compassion. Where differences in specific beliefs and issues occur, you are asked to adopt a "meta-belief stance"—a mental position that allows you to move beyond the divisiveness plaguing the world today. Disagreements and misunderstandings are best resolved in a state of mind that is void of judgment, and respectful of others' freedom of choice.

Chapter Three

Belief-Energy-Action Dynamics

> *Martyrdom has always been a proof of the intensity, never the correctness, of a belief.*
> ~Arthur Schnitzler

Mostly, we run on autopilot, making our choices and taking actions based on the sum total of the beliefs, images, and thought patterns we have acquired from our past experiences, social conditioning, family, relatives, and media. Many of these beliefs have never been examined under the bright light of our global connection to others.

The Power of Beliefs

Beliefs are the solid convictions we hold about ourselves, others, social issues, events, and life. Beliefs differ from opinions in their energy force. The stronger the belief, i.e., the more it's been reinforced mentally or experientially, the more likely it is to elicit our feelings and emotions.

Our beliefs permeate every aspect of our lives, affecting us as individuals, along with all aspects of society.

Turned outward, a person's flawed beliefs can lead to anger, domestic violence, or cowardly hate crimes, such as when radical religious beliefs precipitate suicide bombings and terrorist attacks. Turned inward, faulty beliefs and unsound thinking habits can result in despair, depression, and even suicide. It has been well documented that persons who are seriously depressed hold a battery of emotion-laden beliefs such as "life will never get any better", "it's useless to go on", and "there's no point in trying." These beliefs trigger the feelings of profound despair and depression.

At a community, state, and national level, individual and dominant public beliefs influence and determine policies and laws concerning all sorts of issues—the operation of prison systems, capital punishment, the environment, recycling, global warming, and how the homeless are treated. On an international level, beliefs determine foreign policies and practices. All of which in turn affect our collective well-being. Beliefs hold great power for the shape of our lives and world.

Beliefs Are Learned

No one is born with beliefs about anything. We learn them in the course of living. Core beliefs often originate within our family, schools, religious institutions, and culture. We are influenced by the media, friends, and personal experiences. Although we all like to think we're the authors of our beliefs, and make our own independent choices, in reality, we can only act out of our mind's content. And our slice of life's experiences—no matter how well-educated, well-informed, rational, or well-traveled we are—is extremely limited from a whole-world information perspective.

Even if we had ten thousand lifetimes, we could not assimilate all the information and knowledge available. Nor could we have all the possible experiences. And our tiny sliver of reality can and does teach lies. Though we tend to see our own personal beliefs as facts, even as truths, they are nothing more and nothing less than working hypotheses, subject to constant flux and modification as we gain new information and experiences. That being said, some individual and cultural beliefs result in a better quality of life than others.

Resistance to Change

The problem is that our beliefs are often entrenched so strongly in our identities and how we see ourselves, we feel that if we give them up, we're losing a part of who we are. This is especially true for some of our deep religious beliefs and those we hold on social issues. Beliefs pertaining to abortion, gun control, capital punishment, cloning, and lifestyle differences can trigger strong emotions and actions. When someone attacks our beliefs, we feel like they're attacking us.

Confronted with any beliefs that run counter to our own, we may shut down; we don't want to hear them or even know about them. This is one of the reasons prejudices and irrational beliefs persist even in the face of strong factual evidence that refutes them. We get trapped in our long-held beliefs and thought patterns.

Beliefs Are Mind Tools

We need to take a mental step back, and recognize that our ideas, opinions, thoughts, and beliefs are all just tools of the mind—mechanisms that have evolved for our survival. Ironically, many of these long-held, cherished beliefs are corroding society and that very survival. A deeper understanding of how our beliefs are formed, why they persist, and how they influence behavior, will help move us past intercultural communication barriers that are thwarting constructive change, global well-being, and survival. Discovering how to better use the elements of your mind will result in both self and global empowerment. Learning to appreciate the connection between our beliefs and consequences, will aid in a healthy reappraisal of them.

Beliefs serve an important function in our life by helping us to explain and make sense of the world. They answer questions of why, and, when they are on track, can guide us in useful directions. They have the power to improve the quality of our lives. At our present stage of human development and evolution, at least, we seem to be unable to function without our battery of beliefs. One psychological study has suggested that even when we *knowingly* have misinformation, we will construct beliefs, form opinions, and act on the faulty information.

Beliefs and Truth

> *Human beings are perhaps never more frightening than when they are convinced beyond doubt that they are right.*
> ~Laurens van der Post

It's easy to confuse our core beliefs with truth, and even argue that they have come to us from some higher power. The problem with this is there's no universal consensus of beliefs about what's right or wrong, moral or immoral. We read different books, attend different schools, are exposed to different parenting practices—in short, we become who we are as a result of our cultures, socialization, and experiences. Though we can arrive at common threads of beliefs across cultures—a good thing—it is the flawed, conflicting beliefs that separate us.

Beliefs are a human phenomenon, just a mind resource, and have nothing to do with any ultimate truth. Beliefs are "made up," shifting and changing over time as we acquire new evidence, information, and insights. It's only when we're able to escape from our beliefs that we enter into a realm that might be called Truth.

Truth lies in the realm of being beyond our personally held beliefs, opinions, ideas, and judgments. Truth is in the space between our beliefs and an inner awareness and state of mind that holds no attachment to personal beliefs. Outside the dogma of beliefs, we find love, pure joy, peace, timelessness, and eternity. A number of important books today advocate tapping into this inner realm (the silence, the source, our higher selves) to live our lives. As promising as this sounds, alas, at our present stage of development, we still need the crutch of our beliefs to conduct our affairs. It is from our network of beliefs that our social structures are built—our family systems, as well as our government, schools, military, and economic institutions. The structures of society in turn change as our beliefs change.

This is a call to start viewing your beliefs and thoughts as tools of the mind, not as who you are or as some ultimate Truth. The idea is to increase your repertoire of those empowering beliefs that align with your innate wisdom and goodness—and to learn how to use these tools of the mind more effectively for a better life and world.

> *Whoever undertakes to set himself up as a judge of Truth and Knowledge is shipwrecked by the laughter of the gods.*
> *~Albert Einstein*

You Are the Proprietor and Director of Your Mind's Elements

The happy news is: *you* are the director of your beliefs, thinking, and thoughts. Flawed beliefs preventing you from fulfilling your individual dreams can be changed. And the collective beliefs of all nations' people, determining whether our global community is healthy or unhealthy, prosperous or poor, can also be changed. We have the power to improve our mental makeup in ways that ultimately, collectively, will result in a better world for all humankind.

As our beliefs evolve, our choices and actions evolve, as does the society in which we live. And the more you learn about how much power you have as an individual, the faster these changes will take place. But I'm jumping ahead of myself; before you begin building your bank of empowering beliefs and taking effective action, you must ask yourself,

- What do I want?
- If I could create the life and world of my choice, what would it be?
- From my perspective, what are the core ingredients of a meaningful, rich, fulfilling life?

Depending on your responses to these questions, you will discover the path right for you in fulfilling your quest of purpose.

In the next chapter, you start Step 1 of your journey by developing your unique personal-global vision. Holding a personal vision of your desires and dreams for a better life and world will keep you focused and on track when Murphy's Law strikes and everything goes wrong.

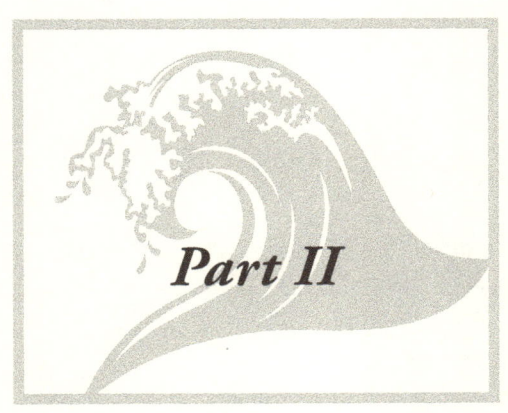

Get Started and Get Excited:
Create Your Personal-Global Vision
Steps 1, 2, 3

> *The first step toward creating an improved future is developing the ability to envision it.*
> ~Author Unknown

> *Visualize this thing you want. See it, feel it, believe in it. Make your mental blueprint and begin.*
> ~Robert Collier

Chapter Four
Step 1

Dream the Life & World You Desire!

Nothing happens unless first a dream.
~Carl Sandburg

Dream life the way you'd like it to be;
then act in the direction of your dream.
~Juanita Louise Vance

Creating a Master Vision

Before you begin building your bank of empowering beliefs, you need to have a clear vision of your personal-global mission, i.e., what are the desired outcomes and in what ways will they make a difference in your life and the lives of others. Without a heartfelt dream and vision of how your sustained efforts can truly make a difference, you will have little motivation and commitment to take action or carry on when things go wrong.

Each of us arrived on Planet Earth for a reason. You are not an accident of birth, nor is life meaningless. Your true purpose—your mission in life—aligns with the universe's purpose, which embodies the qualities of abundance, compassion, beauty, creativity, and reverence for life.

Within our purpose, we are drawn to explore the best within ourselves and others. Living life as a global being, we are in harmony with nature and seek a lifestyle that sustains the welfare of our human family around the world.

When you consciously commit to your deeper purpose, you gain a perspective that keeps you on the path of the greater good, albeit fully engaged in day-to-day events. Your heart and mind respond to the challenges at hand within a larger global framework.

What is your vision?

Probe your heart and mind about what changes you personally would like to see in your life, in others, and in the world. What unique experiences and talents do you have that can enrich others' lives? If you could create any scenario for yourself, what would you be doing? What kind of events would fill your days? What activities are the most meaningful for you? What is the greatest gift you have to give the world? How does the way you spend your time, money, and energy mesh with your deepest values?

Jot down your ideas in the space on the next page to start giving form to your vision. I have written my vision as a sample. However, my vision is not yours, and should only be used as a springboard for your own thoughts. For your vision to have energy and power in your life, it must come from you, and from the heart. It needn't be eloquent or elaborate. In fact, the simpler, the better. Do this now. You will have the opportunity to modify your vision as we proceed.

> *Your vision will become clear only when you look into your heart.*
> *~ Carl Jung*

Sample Vision Statement:

I will do my best to live every aspect of my discretionary time in a way that sustains and promotes global prosperity, education, good communication, social-economic justice, spiritual growth, and creative expression. To me, this means creating a lifestyle that is globally responsible in all areas of my life—as a consumer and investor, in social activities, volunteer work, and relationships. My passion is to empower others accordingly, through writing books, facilitating classes, and by example.

My vision encompasses living in the moment, and continued learning through research, seminars, reading, and open discussion. Along with regular personal assessments to appraise the gap between ideal and actual behaviors, and help me make appropriate changes. I accept my limitation, my many mistakes, and view them as an opportunity for personal growth and development.

More specific activities contained within the umbrella of my mission/vision include daily reflective beach walks, listening to beautiful music, expressive movement, playing with ideas, and spending time with family, friends, and colleagues.

Activity No. 1
Draft Your Master Vision Statement: _____
_____
_____
_____
_____
_____
_____
_____
_____
_____
_____
_____
_____

Remember, your vision needs to be stated in terms of desired outcomes. If you currently are experiencing a problem in your life or feeling the heartache of widespread world suffering, shift your focus to a vision woven from new potentials and possibilities. Exercise your imagination and begin to have a vision of ideal end results. This will help lift your spirits and move you past problems to solutions.

At a later time, you'll want to refine your vision to include the *process* of change toward positive outcomes, i.e., the succession of action patterns that will need to occur in order to arrive at new destinations. Your vision statement is not static, but rather a fluid, dynamic process—shifting and changing as you gather new information and insights.

Review your vision regularly, at least once a day. It is helpful to begin and end your day reviewing your vision statement. *One to two minutes of your time is all it takes!* This will give energy to your daily activities, and keep you from being swallowed up in wasteful, random activities that fall outside your purpose.

When our individual minds are transformed and become open to new visions, the world also commences its transformation. As we collectively solidify our visions of prosperity, cooperation, harmony, and justice, then global conditions change accordingly.

Your purpose and vision are the umbrella under which your goals lie. Types of goals include short-, intermediate-, and long-term. They might also be categorized as essential goals and empowerment goals. Examples of essential goals would be meeting basic security and financial needs, such as living in a safe environment, having a roof over your head, enough food to eat, and adequate healthcare. Empowerment goals would be having opportunities for learning, creative expression, and service to others. Those of us blessed with having our essential goals met have an added responsibility to ourselves and others.

Each person from every far corner of the world has an intrinsic, creative yearning to reach beyond the boundaries of his immediate environment, and take on the challenge and urgent global calling for new ways of thinking, innovative strategies, and solutions that address the tough issues of widespread poverty, warfare, and social-economic injustices. Our innate connection to the whole acts to preserve humanity and the universe of which we are a part. Consciously reaffirming this connection and purpose strengthens our health and well-being.

Once you have drafted a vision in keeping with your values, purpose, and interests, you are ready to move on to Step 2.

> *Where your gifts and your joy meet the*
> *needs of the world, there lies your purpose.*
> *~Dick Leider*

Chapter Five
Step 2
Target Areas for Change

Change has a considerable psychological impact on the human mind. To the fearful it is threatening because it means that things may get worse. To the hopeful it is encouraging because things may get better. To the confident it is inspiring because the challenge exists to make things better.
~King Whitney Jr.

Discretionary Time/Energy Use

In this step, you begin identifying dimensions of your life in which you'd like to see some improvement. A richly fertile area for generating positive personal and global change lies in those hours after work, your discretionary time. It is a time when you're freest to be yourself, and not subject to the demands of an employer.

Although we have many demands on our discretionary time, we always have a choice about how it is divided among our various activities. We go shopping, do our banking, entertain ourselves, visit with friends, participate in family activities, go on vacations, provide for our health needs, and if we have any time or money left, may do volunteer work, donate to worthy causes, and take classes to further our education. Collectively, all these activities have a tremendous impact on us as individuals and on the world. Our choices in this vital segment of our life can enrich or impede our personal and global well-being.

Up for Grabs

Unfortunately, with little formal or informal education in how we can best put all the pieces of our leisure time together for our personal and collective well-being, it is often up for grabs by powerful commercial interests who may have private agendas counterproductive to our personal-global welfare. Or, if we have been living on the fringes of our true mission in life, it is easy to get caught up in passive entertainment and activities that leave us feeling empty and unfulfilled. Surveys have shown that the vast majority of us, even with our crowded calendars, admit to wasting up to 40 percent of our discretionary time in activities such as waiting in lines, watching television, inefficient shopping, and aimlessly reading the newspaper or internet surfing. Capturing those minutes and hours that slip away has the potential to transform your life and keep you anchored on the path of prosperity.

Making Your Leisure Count

Ideally, as global citizens, we would arrange our free time in a way that is consistent with both our individual values and universal values. Indeed, the ambitious aim of this book is to do exactly that! Once you come to a fuller understanding of the power of your daily choices and actions, you are ready to begin charting those personal changes for the creation of a better life and world.

This isn't a call to be perfect and to make perfect choices. If you simply decide on one area of your free time for improvement, this in itself is a vital step toward a better world.

> *One little person, giving all of her time to peace, makes news. Many people, giving some of their time, can make history.*
> *~Peace Pilgrim*

Discretionary Time Dimensions for Improvement

Dimensions of your nonwork time that you might consider for improvement are your personal relationships, physical/mental health, financial fitness, spiritual growth, continued learning, volunteering, and vacation activities.

Embracing an expanded worldview as a global citizen, empowering changes to entertain are your choices as a socially responsible consumer and investor. For example, as a consumer, you may wish to start using your purchasing power to support those corporations which create safe and positive work conditions for their employees, give back to the community, and consider the environmental impact of their products and practices. As an investor, you might want to consider how your hard-earned dollars are being used by your financial institutions. Are they supporting a global corporation which has sweatshops in Third World countries where employees are not paid enough even to purchase clean water? Are they supporting firms notorious for human rights' abuses? Is your money inadvertently aiding destruction of the environment and other things you value?

How do the monetary policies and decisions of your bank, credit card company, internet service provider, and long-distance telephone carrier align with your values? Until I started researching this book, I didn't have a clue about many of these matters. I'm guessing you may not either. In a later section, you'll be given specific and simple actions you can take, in each of these areas, to generate positive results. And, as you'll see, your personal prosperity and financial fitness are intimately tied to the choices you make in these vital areas.

Important categories for improvement for many of us are the volunteer work we do in our community and our charity donations to organizations. With limited time and energy available, we'd like to be certain our efforts are best serving our local and global communities. We want to know that our charity dollars are being responsibly managed and distributed to the proper recipients. We'd like to be assured that the money put into our banks and other financial institutions is wisely invested in those things we cherish: education, freedom, fair-trade practices, justice, and equal opportunities.

Perhaps you'd like to broaden your friendship links to persons in other countries to improve global communication and understanding, but are not sure where to begin. Or you'd like to see freedom of education spread throughout the world, but are unclear about what role you might play here.

Activity No. 2

List in the space below three to six dimensions of your leisure time in which you'd like to see some improvement:

_____
_____
_____
_____
_____
_____
_____
_____

Target Areas For Change

In these first steps, the idea is not to know *how* to go about creating change, only to consider the possibilities, to mindstorm, and play around with different visions. Give thought to what you'd *like* to see at this stage, without clogging up your mind with all the obstacles, or problems of making that vision a reality.

Plant in your mind the seed that you can create whatever beauty in the world you can imagine. Actually, start to see it in your mind's eye. See the possibilities, the end results, and set your mind to act as if they had already begun to happen. In reality, they have. As soon as we set in motion the images and intention, an energy builds to make them manifest in the world. Allow your imagination to soar, and know that you have the power to make your dreams come true!

> *Imagination is more important than knowledge.*
> *-Albert Einstein*

Chapter Six
Step 3
Map Out Your Personal-Global Dreams

*Those who say it can't be done are
usually interrupted by others doing it.*
-Joel A. Barker

Refine and Focus Your Vision and Dream

According to your values, what do you see as most important? Which are fundamental to your master vision? Prosperity? Building good relationships? Health? Education? You should work on no more than three goals at a time. If you identified six different goals, you need to consider which ones are most important to you now. This will depend on your current situation, personality, and special interests. Without a clear picture of your goals, it is impossible to keep your vision before you. We'll take three examples that fall within the realm of discretionary time to use as a prototype for our discussion: *Personal-Global Prosperity, Communication and Understanding,* and *Education.*

While at first glance such grand categories would appear too monumental and unwieldy even to consider, later we'll look at specific actions you can take to generate positive change in each area. Using a broad paintbrush at this juncture lets you see the abundant range of opportunities in which you might act as a change agent while simply going about your daily routine. Use the discussions in this section as a catalyst for your own ideas. What kinds of activities are most compatible with your own desires and dreams?

After each goal statement below, I'd like you to ponder the ways you could make it a reality. In another step, you'll be given dozens of different actions from which to select; however, it's always best first to use your own imagination and creative thinking to reflect on possible ways to bring a goal to life.

Goal Category #1: Personal-Global Prosperity

So long as the increased wealth which modern progress brings goes but to build up great fortunes, to increase luxury and make sharper the contrast between the House of Have and the House of Want, progress is not real and cannot be permanent.
~ Henry George

Personal Prosperity and true happiness are intimately tied to taking global responsibility. The rugged individualism and self-interest that brought wealth to many in the past are no longer viable in the interdependent world we share today. Without consideration for the welfare of our whole human family, our progress is in serious jeopardy. To provide a better world for our children, grandchildren, and future generations, it is mandatory that we begin adopting a global perspective. This needn't entail making painful sacrifices or enduring personal hardships. Each of us has a role to play according to our particular circumstances. Your personality and heartfelt desires will dictate the direction and choices that are right for you. Kindness and service to others bring self-enrichment and spiritual growth. In unison, through an expanded shift in thinking and awareness, a new world based on compassion, trust, and cooperation will emerge to benefit all.

Global Prosperity can be defined as a world in which every person has access to clean water to drink, enough food to eat, and shelter from harsh weather conditions. Further, it is a world that flourishes, one of good fortune and riches. It does not necessarily imply living in mansions, having expensive cars, tons of gadgets, and streets lined with shopping malls. Simple living quarters, clean fresh air to breathe, a garden of fruit and flowers, and peace of mind, would be heaven on earth for the millions of people in Third World countries suffering from disease, starvation, and lack of security.

Any definition of prosperity must also comprise equitable rights and opportunities for each member of society, irrespective of gender, race, age, religion, rank, or lifestyle orientation. It must include women and children, the disadvantaged, and the elderly.

A culture's prosperity should be measured by how well it provides for the most vulnerable and marginal members of society—*not* by how well it accommodates the rich and influential. Creating a prosperous, harmonious society is more than just a matter of economic development; it is about human development and nourishing the potential of each person. Once basic needs are met, personal-global prosperity is about *being* more, not *having* more.

> *Much violence is based on the illusion that life*
> *is a property to be defended and not to be shared.*
> ~ Henri Nouwen

Activity No. 3

Reflect on your role in aiding Global Prosperity. Helping others to get what they want helps you get what you want. What specific goals would you especially like to see transpire? List your ideas in the space below:

_____
_____
_____
_____
_____
_____
_____
_____
_____
_____

Goal Category #2: Communication and Understanding

Man is always inclined to be intolerant towards the thing, or person, he hasn't taken the time adequately to understand.
~Robert R. Brown

Building relationships through good communication skills begins at home and in your community. Interpersonal family flare-ups, unresolved conflicts, and angry confrontations, damage our mental, spiritual, and physical health. Poor communication practices distance us from each other and contribute to racism and domestic violence. Listening to learn, and respecting others in spite of differences, will go a long way to improve communication and reduce misunderstandings. Practicing good relationships at home is the basis for improved relationships internationally.

A working definition of good global communication is searching for common needs, values, and goals across cultures. Some of the commonalities most cultures share are concern for their families, the desire to live in peace, and the yearning to make the world a better place for their children and grandchildren. We can avoid adversarial confrontations by actively listening to others' viewpoints and having a mind open to differences.

Keeping an open mind doesn't mean acceptance of different views for oneself. Simply listening to the other person's point of view, to the extent that you can start to see the world through her eyes, is a fundamental step toward understanding. Expressing feelings and dissimilar viewpoints within a context of mutual respect leaves the door open for amiable mutual influence and constructive action.

Learning good communication skills is the foundation on which global trust and understanding are built. Using good communication skills in our contacts with individuals in other countries can help build common goals, improve relationships, and reduce intercultural misunderstandings. In the process, we will make new friends, perhaps learn to think in new ways, explore different ways of doing things, and experience the joys of a new adventure.

In the 21ˢᵗ century, what creates peace is not governments, or religions, or nations, or individual leaders. What creates peace is you. Through your bright hopes, your efforts, and your belief in peace, you can create peace and harmony for yourself, your family, your country, your environment, and the world.
~Masami Saionji

Activity No. 4
Think about what specific goals you'd like to see accomplished that will improve personal-global communication and understanding. Jot these down below:

_____
_____
_____

_____
_____
_____
_____
_____
_____
_____

Goal Category #3: Education

Education is "the movement from darkness to light.
~Allan Bloom

Education in our changing world is a lifelong process. Obtaining a high school diploma or college degree is not the end of education, but the beginning. Both formal education taught in schools and informal education through exposure to reliable information, aid our growth and development. Especially critical to our survival is an education that gives us a healthy appreciation of the individual-global connection, and the power of personal choice.

Our greatest hope for creating positive global change is through the educational process. We need an educational curriculum not just of the three Rs, but one that teaches kindness and compassion for the human family and our planet—an education that takes into account our cultural and ethnic differences and teaches us to appreciate, grow, and learn from each other. Education must also include skills in nonviolent conflict resolution, parenting practices, and issues of gender, rank and race. Schools and the media need to have stronger voices for individual global responsibility.

Early education is of paramount importance. Children reflect what they read in their schoolbooks and what they learn from their classmates and teachers. If teachers use physical punishment, exhibit racism, or prevent students from expressing their ideas and opinions, this will become part of those students' repertoire of behaviors.

Education of children must begin with each of us—as parents, grandparents, aunts, uncles, and teachers. Only then can we set an example for our children and ward off prejudices and violence. Young children also need to be taught communication skills, nonviolent conflict resolution, values, and respect for other races and cultures. Selecting books, films, and games that instill these values for the children in our lives is something each of us can offer.

Sound education cultivates an attitude of mutual respect in spite of differences, and moves us away from flawed beliefs that breed gender or racial supremacy and revenge practices.

> *Only the educated are free.*
> *~Epictetus*

Activity No. 5

From the standpoint of your interests, skills, and personality, ponder what steps you could take to begin making this vision a reality. Consider both your personal and global educational goals. List these in the space below:

_____
_____
_____
_____
_____
_____
_____
_____
_____
_____
_____
_____

Note: *Describe your personal-global goals according to the values you hold, keeping them clear, colorful, and specific. This will give your vision power.*

When jotting down actions you might take for the above goals, also be sure and state them in the present tense, in positive terms, and according to *what you want*, not what you don't want.

Freedom from debt is not a goal. Freedom from poverty is not a goal. Prosperity and success are goals. Ending war is not a goal. Nonviolence and peaceful resolution are goals. Ending illiteracy is not a goal. Universal education is a goal. This is much more than just a semantic distinction. Your vision needs to be focused on the *desired results* for it to become a reality. Remember, what you focus on expands. You want to keep your vision of possibilities and potentials, not problems! Strive to hold your vision steadily and unswervingly. A collective sustainable vision will mold and move the world toward those ideals we cherish. *Dream the life and world you desire!*

Part III

CHALLENGES TO CHANGE
BREAK FREE FROM BELIEF BARRIERS
FOILING YOUR DREAMS
STEP 4

"Believe it can be done. When you believe something can be done, really believe, your mind will find the ways to do it. Believing a solution paves the way to solution."
~David J. Schwartz

"To accomplish great things, we must not only act, but also dream; not only plan, but also believe."
~Anatole France

In the next chapters, we'll look at flawed beliefs that interfere with achieving your dreams for a better life and world. More important, in this step you'll learn how you can begin displacing them with empowering beliefs that will move you toward a brighter future for yourself and others. Remember, as you change your own beliefs and thoughts, a part of humanity changes also. Dissolving the doubts, and limiting "it-can't-be-done" beliefs, propels us forward.

Some of the beliefs I'll be presenting to you may be difficult for you to accept immediately. That is normal and as it should be. Question, reflect, and ponder the new ideas before adopting them. Recall that beliefs are only tools of the mind—hypotheses that change as new evidence presents itself. See them as links to your experiences. Then ask which ones will best serve you and humanity.

Chapter Seven

Banish Belief Barriers Preventing Effective Action

To believe a thing is impossible is to make it so.
- French Proverb

Belief Barriers

Your first task in this step is to identify any Belief Barriers that are standing between you and your goals and objectives. Belief Barriers put up a wall in your mind that prevents new ideas, new visions, and new solutions from entering:

- You're pursuing a foolish pipe dream, unrealistic and impossible.
- It's not viable.
- It can't be done.
- There'll always be poverty in the world.
- There'll always be the weak and lazy who don't get ahead.
- The world is made up of the good guys and the bad guys.

- Wars are inevitable.
- There'll always be social and economic injustices.
- It's never been done before.
- We tried that and it didn't work.

You've heard them all. We've heard them so many times and for so long, they've become self-fulfilling. No wonder we believe them!

Belief Barriers prevent us from transforming our values and ideals into actions. Think of Belief Barriers as analogous to the Berlin or China Walls—big and impenetrable. New ideas, visions, and solutions are unable to enter. And the more Belief Barriers we have, the more solid the mental wall.

But the Berlin Wall came down and the Great Wall of China no longer keeps anyone in or out. And the hard, brutal wall built from the bricks of Belief Barriers, holding us back from a personal-global world of prosperity, social-economic justice, and cooperation, can come down as well. Our minds are the last great frontier to be explored, understood, and changed. Our long tragic history of man's inhumanity to man, wars, poverty, injustices, and suffering, is not going to end because a messiah comes to rescue us; it's finally going to crumble because we've learned how to change our minds effectively.

The solid wall built of Belief Barriers *is* going to come down, and, when that happens, our hearts will start connecting with the hearts of others, true communication will flow, our visions will come alive as real possibilities, and a new world will blossom. Already, the wellspring of timid hope is swelling, and our hearts are opening to song. Out of the darkness, a vibrant new rhythm is embracing our planet and pulling us toward the bonds of peace and prosperity.

Idealism, however, must be grounded in practicality. We look now at some common Belief Barriers frequently voiced by my students and clients concerning their use of discretionary time and the task of creating positive change. Most of these center around time limitations, issues of responsibility, whether individual efforts truly make a difference, and uncertainty about how to get started. Though many of these beliefs and rebuttals are obvious, even cliché, it is important to make your convictions explicit. If they remain as ill-thought-out fragments lingering below the surface of your awareness, they tie up energy and prevent constructive action.

Take a few minutes to reflect on the five Belief Barriers discussed below. The majority of us hold one or more of these flawed beliefs. Then make a conscious effort to open your mind to the new empowering beliefs. Allow yourself to suspend any judgments about whether they're right or wrong, accurate or inaccurate. In a later chapter, we'll explore "convincers"—supporting statements and rationales for the new empowering beliefs. For now, the idea is to set your mind's stage for sweeping away any flawed beliefs undermining personal-global well-being.

Belief Barrier #1

- **Discouragement, self-doubts, and frustration**

    "Nothing I do seems to bring about much improvement or prosperity in my life. I work hard, am honest, and a good citizen, but it doesn't seem to make any difference."

Empowering Belief:

Your choices and actions matter regardless of the outcome! While you do not always see immediate tangible results, perseverance in the direction of your dreams and goals will ultimately attract prosperity and happiness. The key is believing in yourself and your goals, and following through to completion.

Belief Barrier #2
- Too many worries and obligations in my personal affairs to attend to global concerns

    "It's all I can do to take care of myself, much less worry about the rest of the world's problems. Besides, there's no way I can add anything else to my schedule. I don't have any energy left at the end of the day."

Empowering Belief:
It isn't necessary to add any additional obligations to your schedule. Many of the actions that are listed in Step 5 are things you're already doing, e.g., shopping, banking, and going on vacation. Indeed, some of the suggested actions may well *increase* your time and energy! You'll be asked to revisit and possibly change some of your consumer, investment, and entertainment choices—*not* add more to your schedule.

Worry burns up energy and is counterproductive. By taking a few simple, concrete actions, you'll be contributing to global well-being and also enriching your personal life.

> *Action is worry's worst enemy.*
> ~ Proverb

Belief Barrier #3
- **Abdication of personal responsibility**

    "It's not my responsibility to solve the weighty problems of the world. I take care of my family. I volunteer in the community and give to my church and charities. I didn't create the problem. Why should I take responsibility for solving it?"

Empowering Belief:
Each of us is responsible for creating a better world. The idea isn't that you

perform any one giant feat to improve the world, only that we make the best choices possible from where we currently stand.

Adopting this belief strengthens awareness of the ways in which our day-to-day choices can impede or improve global prosperity, universal education, and understanding.

There is no doubt that such lofty ideals as global prosperity, education, and understanding appear as momentous and insurmountable undertakings from where we stand as individuals, especially looking at the giant obstacles we face. We need to remind ourselves, however, that every worthwhile accomplishment first started in someone's imagination.

As powerless as you may feel to change the course of events, today, perhaps more than at any other time in history, there is a need for each of us to take individual responsibility for creating a better world. We cannot assume that the government, nongovernment organizations, or someone else in a position of power will respond with compassion, caring, and the needed expertise or services to solve the serious problems that face our world today. Each person is ultimately responsible and culpable for the state of the world.

If not you, who???

> *If all of us acted in unison as I act individually, there would be no wars and no poverty. I have made myself personally responsible for the fate of every human being who has come my way.*
> ~Anais Nin

Belief Barrier #4

- **Doubts about my ability to create positive change or influence the course of events**

    "I find it hard to believe that my efforts will make any real difference, or that my little day-to-day choices are having any major impact on the big problems of the world."

Empowering Belief:
The cumulative impact of millions of individual actions can result in a host of community and global problems—or create solutions to those problems.

Although many of us would like to make a difference in the world, solutions to the weighty problems of war, crime, poverty, and injustice can seem far removed from our private worlds. Yet, each of us in our own way *does* have the power to change positively the course of events. You don't have to be a Mother Teresa, Mohandas Gandhi, or Martin Luther King, Jr. A full-time commitment and sacrifice of personal and family goals are unrealistic for most of us, and totally unnecessary. What *is* realistic is educating ourselves about how our daily consumer, banking, transportation, vacation, and entertainment choices cumulatively have a huge impact on the world. For example:

- Your consumer purchases may be unwittingly supporting an unethical corporate conglomerate running Third World sweatshops in which thousands of women and children are paid subsistence wages and work fifteen-hour days. For example, at this writing, Nike pays women in Indonesia *seventeen cents an hour*—even lower than wages in Thailand and India.

- The bank where you have your checking and savings accounts may be using your funds to invest in alcohol and tobacco companies that are targeting our youth.

- The household cleaning products you use may be undermining the safety of your family and community.

- The airlines and cars you use could be contributing to the serious problem of global warming, and the depletion of natural resources.

- Your entertainment choices for movies and television could be supporting programs adding to youth violence and crime.

- The cosmetics, hair sprays, and deodorants so many of us purchase may be supporting companies which do animal testing—maiming and killing dogs and cats.

- Failure to inform ourselves about the distribution practices of the charities we so generously make donations to, may result in our hard-earned dollars inadvertently being spent in ways we did not intend, and diverting needed money from more socially responsible charities.

- Your failure to vote or influence others to vote may tip the scale in favor of an unqualified candidate.

Individually, our consumer choices and purchases would seem to have little impact on the world at large. It's our credit cards that we run up, and our lives that suffer if we overspend or make unwise purchases and investments. It's our minds and bodies that suffer if we overdose on passive or violent television and internet entertainment. Nonetheless, the end result of our collective choices and actions adds up to big waves of change that can bring us closer together as a world, or move us farther apart.

This is not an attempt to have you overhaul your whole lifestyle—only to open your mind and heart to the larger picture of humanity, and begin making the connection between your individual choices and global change. When we become conscious of the tremendous impact our cumulative choices have on humanity's fate, we become energized and excited about the mighty power of each and every one of our decisions and actions.

To get you started in the direction of making those choices that support positive global change and better world understanding, begin looking at your daily habits through global eyes. Are the products you purchase supporting a business enterprise that is having a detrimental effect on people in your community or elsewhere? Are your entertainment choices promoting a healthier mental and physical climate for everyone? How much of your time is spent in leisure pursuits and volunteer activities that are consistent with your values? Are any of your consumer choices inadvertently aiding businesses and organizations that carry out practices deleterious to the peoples and environment of the world? Is your communication with persons of other races or cultures unwittingly widening the gaps of misunderstanding, distrust, and division among nations?

Each of us has *way* more power than we give ourselves credit for. I urge you to step up to your position of power, and begin to make your choices and take your actions within the context of a whole-world view. Even if we only incorporate one small change into our lives each week or month, this will have a ripple effect, making a difference in our own well-being and that of many, many others. One action a week equals fifty-two actions a year. Multiply this by a million people acting for a better world, and that's a mighty force.

> *The question for each person to settle is not what he would do if he had the means, time, influence and educational advantages, but what he will do with the things he has.*
> *~ Hamilton Wright Mabee*

Belief Barrier #5

- **Feeling overwhelmed**

    "I feel overwhelmed by all the problems in the world today. It's too painful and too much for me to think about. I don't know where to begin. Besides, I have my own problems to worry about."

Empowering Belief:
Take the weight off your shoulders. You don't have to do everything. A common feeling is being overwhelmed by the enormity of the poverty, suffering, and illnesses plaguing our world. Continuing wars, violence, injustices, sex trafficking of children . . . it's an endless list. From the individual standpoint, it's hard to know where to begin.

I suggest that you start from the stance of your personal values. As you review the actions in the chapters ahead, ask yourself where your interests and skills lie. Remind yourself that you needn't do everything. Make your choices to act within the scope of your vision statement. What small act can you perform for global humanity that aligns with your personal goals, lifestyle, and dreams? That is all you need ever do—nothing more, nothing less. As author Peter Marshall reminded us, "Small deeds done are better than great deeds planned."

When I was considering this question for myself, I chose to give the bulk of my time and energy to those activities that are preventive measures for long-term and permanent change, rather than trying to treat symptoms. Doing research, writing, lecturing, and educating others on how positive change occurs through individual efforts was consistent with my daily routine and lifestyle as a psychology instructor, author, and educator. I thought that, if I could help others become more aware of how their everyday choices impact the world, along with giving them the mental tools for taking effective actions, this would lead to a broader citizenship equipped for meeting global needs. Insofar as possible, I encourage you to focus on action strategies that address the root causes of poverty and intercultural disharmony, rather than the symptoms.

> *We ourselves feel that what we are doing is just a drop in the ocean. But the ocean would be less because of that missing drop.*
> ~Mother Teresa

Activity No. 6
Shedding Beliefs Preventing You from Taking Effective Action toward Personal-Global Empowerment

What personal beliefs do you hold that are preventing you from taking effective action? List these below. Next, induce their displacement with a new more empowering belief. Cross out the old belief.

_____
_____
_____
_____
_____
_____
_____
_____
_____
_____
_____
_____
_____
_____
_____

Please don't skip these exercises. Engaging your thought and emotion in the activities confirms your commitment and acceptance of personal responsibility for constructive change. Ultimately it is you who will make a difference. And, if you have read this far, congratulations! You are well on the way to improving our troubled world—and your own life in the process!

Chapter Eight

Stamp Out Beliefs That Are Limiting Prosperity

> *Massive poverty and obscene inequality are such terrible scourges of our times—times in which the world boasts breathtaking advances in science, technology, industry and wealth accumulation—that they have to rank alongside slavery and apartheid as social evils.*
> ~Nelson Mandela

Personal Prosperity and Service to Others: The Fallacy of Self-Interest

Acting solely within our own self-interests for personal gain and profit has never been a viable stance. Without creating a product or benefit for others, we are doomed to failure. In today's global economy, it is even more critical that we open our eyes to the greater good and the impact of our daily lifestyle choices on others. We are all interconnected, and conditions of poverty, perilous conflicts, and illiteracy thousands of miles away can affect us in unexpected and unwanted ways—witness recent terrorist attacks. Colin Powell has said, "The war against terror is bound up in the war against poverty." Taking steps to end poverty and injustice is the surest way to cultivate peace.

While acting in our own self-interests may improve the lot of some of us, we lose in the long run. Evading our responsibilities as global citizens because we're not personally starving, in a war zone, or under attack, only postpones our fate, and the fate of our children and grandchildren. We live in a fragile world that needs the care and attention of each and every one of us.

But service to others motivated by concern for our own survival, or out of guilt, is insufficient. We are all part of the body of humanity, and, when one part is in pain or suffering, reaching out to help heals and keeps us healthy. When you offer service to others with no motive other than to help, the rewards are many. Connecting to humanity through unselfish service will result in your own transformation and fulfillment. Compassion for others, whether they are strangers or family, is an innate quality of the soul, and, if we deny it in ourselves or fail to give it expression, we cannot be whole and happy. The dissatisfaction, despair, and unhappiness we see in so many faces of those rich in material goods, stem from not paying attention to this vital aspect of their selves.

Viewing the world through global eyes and acting in the service of others through our discretionary time choices, however, needn't preclude material prosperity. I believe man and woman were intended to be rich—but rich spiritually as well as materially. Our personal desires for prosperity (spiritual and material wealth) must be grounded in a desire for prosperity for everyone. Making those choices that support the wealth of all persons will ensure a safer and saner world. Acting to build a better world for everyone benefits each of us.

Even our small choices can make a big difference in the lives of others. A donation of only two dollars to a child in Afghanistan can buy school supplies for a whole year. One simple act makes the difference between a child growing up in ignorance—and vulnerable to tyrants with ulterior agendas—or gaining the knowledge to empower their own homes and country.

Global Prosperity, Beliefs, and the Deluge of Information

With all the disinformation, confusing statistics, and government and corporate special interest propaganda on resolving the world's dilemmas, it's difficult to separate fact from fiction and to generate viable global visions and solutions—much less know what to do that will make a difference. Preoccupied with our own personal responsibilities and obligations, overwhelmed by the sheer amount of information, in our frustration and confusion, we fall prey to easy answers, myths, and misconceptions—faulty beliefs—that have little substance or veracity. As much as we pride ourselves on being right and in command of "the facts," in many, many areas, we're not, and never could be. But while we can never know everything about everything, we can make a mental shift that allows us to expel critical flawed beliefs that draw us into unwise decisions and actions.

Listed below are just a few beliefs and mindsets that infringe on our objectivity and keep us from realizing greater personal-global prosperity. Which limiting beliefs do you currently hold? How are they influencing your thinking, decision making, and actions? Make an effort to embrace the new beliefs by considering not only the underlying logic and rationale presented for each, but also the consequences.

Remember, beliefs—whether right or wrong, based on facts or hearsay—determine emotions and actions. I'm asking you to consider the impact of your beliefs in terms of your personal-global vision and goals.

If you have a vision of peace and prosperity, ask yourself, what kind of beliefs support this vision? Where does a belief such as "things will never get any better" take you? Where does a belief in "an eye for an eye" lead? Is this what you want? Take charge of the content of your mind, and strive to discharge those beliefs that stand in the way of greater prosperity.

Belief Barrier #1
- Life is mostly up to chance and fate

    "I don't have the contacts, power, education, knowledge, or know-how to change the world. I don't see what I can do."

Empowering Belief:
Both our own lives and the world are constantly changing. Whether those changes empower us and our neighbors depends on our vision, choices, and actions. Each of us in our own way has the power to create positive change. Personal empowerment and planetary empowerment derive from our beliefs and the actions triggered by those beliefs.

Belief Barrier #2
- Lack of confidence in myself and abilities

    "Who am I to help others become more prosperous when my own life is so imperfect?"

Empowering Belief:
The starting point for change is unconditional self-acceptance of where you are now. We all go through different stages in our personal growth. Waiting for self-perfection before acting in the service of others is an untenable stance. We need to make choices and act from where we are *now*. As you begin taking those action steps within the context of "prosperity for all," you'll find that your own personal growth and prosperity will accelerate.

Keeping your vision of personal-global prosperity and manifesting this vision in your day-to-day choices builds a better life and world for all.

Belief Barrier #3

- Confusing self-worth with material wealth

    "I'm only earning $40,000 a year while my neighbor earns twice as much. Something must be wrong with me."

In Western society we're prone to confuse self-worth with net worth. The more money someone has, the more we tend to value her. How rational is this? Professional sports stars earn millions annually, while schoolteachers average well under $100,000 a year. Which is making the greater contribution to our world? Far too many of us put the same value on our own life. We compare ourselves with those who have bigger houses, better cars, fatter bank accounts, and big bucks to spend. If we're not doing as well as the Joneses, something must be wrong with us.

Empowering Belief:

Self-worth is a given. We have value because we are here. It needn't be tied to any criterion. Striving to live according to sound values and principles, however, is a better measure of self-worth than how much money someone has managed to accumulate. As we reflect more on those things that really matter in life—such as family, community, and peaceful coexistence—we are in a position to steer away from conditioned cultural beliefs that tie self-worth to material riches.

Belief Barrier #4

- Scarcity

    "More for you means less for me."

A commonly held Belief Barrier that limits our prosperity is the idea of scarcity—that there's only so much to go around. This is a holdover from early twentieth-century Keynesian economics that taught that the pie of food, shelter, and other resources is limited, and, when we cut it into pieces, some are going to get more and others less. More for you means less for me.

Please read on before you make a judgment here. My point is that we can all live together in greater abundance by attending to the needs of each member of our human family: "To satisfy all the world's sanitation and food requirements would cost only $13 billion, hardly as much as the people of the United States and the European Union spend each year on perfume."[1]

Belief Barrier #5
- **Foreign aid is the answer**

"Increasing foreign aid will solve poverty in the world."

Another misconception is that merely increasing foreign aid will solve the world's poverty problem, when, in fact, much of this money often winds up in the hands of corrupt governments which are failing to instigate reforms that would ease hunger.

In delivering foreign aid, we need to focus on the needs of the poor. Foreign aid to poverty-stricken countries must be spent on health care and promoting universal primary education, with no strings attached. In other words, impoverished citizens need the basic tools that will limit government corruption, and put them in a position to pull themselves up by their own bootstraps.

Belief Barrier #6
- **Natural disasters**

"World poverty is beyond our control."

Another misguided belief is that poverty is largely caused by natural disasters such as droughts and flooding. Although earthquakes, tsunamis, and other natural disasters sometimes have devastating effects, it is the human factor that makes a significant difference in saving lives—our planning and preparedness, compassion, and global responsiveness. The amount of starvation, illness, and deaths is exacerbated mainly by economic and political policies.

Humans, not natural disasters or limited resources, are largely responsible for the preponderance of ongoing poverty and suffering in the world today.

Empowering Belief:
In reality, there's more than enough food to feed—right now—every person on the face of the earth. The problem is not one of scarcity or natural disasters, but one of human policies and distribution.

Facts: Abundance, not scarcity, best describes our food supply. Many countries in which people are starving are actually exporting wheat, rice, and other grains. Indonesia and India are prime examples. Why? A primary reason is that masses of simple farm folks have lost their land to an elite wealthy class and, with it, their livelihoods and buying power. Wealthy landowners have thus found it more profitable to sell their crops abroad.

Even in America, our farmers' huge surplus of crops is well known, although we too have thousands of undernourished people. Food is not in short supply. It has never been so abundant. There is enough right now to provide each person in the world with at least 2,700 calories a day.[2]

That said, we must not become overly confident that the abundance of today will continue indefinitely into the future, nor that shortages can be solved solely by science and technological advances. The current drain on the earth's resources is taking its toll, and we need to act accordingly to preserve our environment.

> *Security can only be achieved through constant change, through discarding old ideas that have outlived their usefulness, and adapting others to current facts.*
> *– William O. Douglas*

Belief Barrier #7

- **The past equals the future**

    "It's always been this way."

Another Belief Barrier is that history repeats itself. There have always been the rich and the poor. There will always be poverty and pain. There will always be the "haves" and the "have-nots." There will always be wars, and the consequent suffering and loss of lives and property.

To explain away the severe poverty and suffering of three-fourths of the human population today (primarily women and children), it is easy to fall into these clichés and false beliefs. Our minds want explanations, and will automatically generate answers out of whatever mind content we happen to have available. We seek answers to *Why did this terrible thing happen?* or *Why do these dreadful situations exist?* And our mind is going to churn out answers to these pressing concerns from its current stockpile of information, impressions, and habitual ways of thinking.

Empowering Belief:

The future can be whatever we decide it to be. The past needn't equal the future. History doesn't necessarily repeat itself. Only when we keep thinking and doing things in the same ways, does this hold true. Consequences are a function of our beliefs and behaviors. When we change our minds and our behaviors, the consequences change. This is true whether we're talking about individual change or global change. *Our past is not our future unless we choose it.*

In fact, the world of the twenty-first century is quite different in many respects from the past. Changes have been made in our world today that people in other eras would never have believed possible.

- Early in history, all primitive cultures practiced human sacrifice. It's been estimated that Aztecs sacrificed fifteen thousand to two-hundred-fifty thousand humans per year to their gods. Rarely do we encounter this dreadful practice today.[3]

- With few exceptions, ancient Greek and Egyptian cultures treated children and women horrifically.

- During the eighteenth century, over 75 percent of all the people living were held in slavery and serfdom. By the end of the nineteenth century, this was completely reversed—slavery had become illegal virtually everywhere.

- During the Middle Ages in Europe, tens of thousands of persons, mostly women, were put to death by fire for "possessing demons." While isolated instances of this abysmal practice are still found in parts of the world, it has otherwise been all but eliminated.

- Apartheid, which suppressed the nonwhite majority in South Africa, ended in a relatively short period of time, thanks to the awareness and efforts of those dedicated to bringing about change.

- The International Criminal Court (ICC) treaty (1998) has been adopted by 120 countries. ICC has the power both to investigate and prosecute individuals accused of crimes against humanity, crimes of war, and genocide, as well as being able to defend the rights of vulnerable persons with little recourse to justice, e.g., millions of women and children in many countries.

- The barbaric practice of capital punishment has now been abolished in ninety-two countries, up from sixteen countries in 1977. As of December 2008, more than two-thirds of the world's nations have abolished the death penalty in law or practice. In spite of the sad failure of the United States here, the world continues to move closer toward universal abolition.[4]

- Public education in many countries has grown dramatically over the years. In most of the developing world, for example, access to primary school has increased sharply, and, in some regions, has approached that in developed countries. Secondary school attendance has also increased rapidly in recent decades.[5] In spite of serious needs for ongoing efforts, progress *is* being made.

- Women's lives in Western countries have improved enormously from earlier periods in history. In Canada's early history, prior to a few steadfast women taking action, a woman was not even considered to be "a person" in the eyes of the law. Women now vote, hold public offices, and have benefits their earlier sisters could only dream about. Women now own or manage close to 50 percent of all private business in the United States. In the past, women were almost totally excluded from politics and finance. It's only been in the twentieth century that they've begun to make some strides.

- A greater partnership between the sexes is evident in many nations today. Certainly there are still many gender-based disparities, and a need to continue our efforts toward eliminating all forms of discrimination, whether based on gender, race, rank, age, ethnic group, lifestyle, disability, or sexual orientation. These conditions will change as we change.

Permanent change rarely comes about quickly or easily. Global public awareness, informed actions, and our commitment to ongoing personal-societal improvements can, and will, lead to greater abundance, cooperation, and understanding throughout the world. Cultivating a sustained vision, and learning how our minds function in support of that vision, will move us forward.

As long as false mindsets arguing *There will always be poverty, injustice, and wars*, persist among the majority of the population, they will continue to be self-fulfilling.

There is no excuse in a civilized society for wars that kill, mutilate, and abuse our human family. There is no excuse for the social and economic disparities that exist in the world today. And there is no excuse for not educating ourselves in the dynamics of mind behavior, and assuming individual responsibility for humanity's plight.

> *Create a vision and never let the environment, other people's beliefs, or the limits of what has been done in the past shape your decisions. Ignore conventional wisdom.*
> *~Anthony Robbins*

Belief Barrier #8

- **Everybody gets what they deserve**

    "She had it coming."

This belief is far more pervasive in society than you might imagine, and is completely unfounded. It has its basis in religious fundamentalism, and has permeated society's thinking in a host of unfortunate ways by blaming the victim. In the Middle Ages in Europe, we saw the burning of tens of thousands of "witches"—mostly innocent young women believed to possess demons.

In America today, over one million annual cases of domestic violence and rape are often explained away with charges of "she provoked him" or "she tantalized him." Since Adam and Eve, the woman has been cast as the temptress, and considered responsible for whatever dreadful fate befalls her: "She must have done something wrong, sinful, or bad for that to happen." In reality, there are many, many innocent victims throughout the world who, through no fault of their own, are subject to poverty, illness, injustice, and hardship.

Empowering Belief:

Everyone in the world deserves a grande life. What is "a grande life"? At the bare minimum, every human has a right to enough food to eat, clean water to drink, and freedom from abuse. Cultivating a personal belief system that allows for the prosperity, abundance, and well-being of all humanity is fundamental to positive change. By nourishing this belief system within ourselves, we will begin to eradicate the damaging belief systems that have prevailed.

We have the resources today, right now, to provide enough food and clean water for every person on this planet. And we have the scientific and technological skills that could provide security from abuse and ensure equitable rights. What we haven't had is the solid belief and trust in ourselves to make these real possibilities. They have variously been dismissed as liberal pipe dreams, pie-in-the-sky ideals, or just plain nonsense. Or, worse, we have shoved them into the far corners of our minds as we get caught up in our own private dramas.

> *Think of all the things thought impossible until they happened.*
> ~Mohandas Gandhi

Belief Barrier #9

- People are poor because they lack willpower or are just naturally lazy, incompetent, or stupid

    "He's always been a lazy good-for-nothing."

Empowering Belief:

Rampant poverty in many countries is due to structural sources—the financial institutions and policies inherent in the community. To cite just one example: Nobel Peace Prize winner Muhammad Yunus, Bangladeshi banker and founder of Grameen Bank, found that by making small microloans—some only a few dollars—to help a family buy a cow, or materials for crafts, sewing materials, bamboo, etc., to start a business, their situation could be reversed from being on the verge of starvation to becoming self-sufficient. Since Grameen's founding in 1976, Yunus has helped millions of individuals help themselves and their families and communities. Their poverty had nothing to do with laziness, willpower, or lack of intelligence. They simply needed capital and human trust to get started.

Grameen Bank's unsecured loans have been given to more than two million poor individuals in Bangladesh, with 95 percent of the loans going to women. Does it work? Do people repay? Yes! There has been an astounding repayment rate of 98 percent to date.[6]

This program has been replicated by other organizations in over fifty countries, helping hundreds of thousands of persons, including some poverty-stricken communities in the United States.

For millions of people around the world, being poor has little or nothing to do with inherent laziness, lack of intelligence, or willpower.

> *Poverty is like punishment*
> *for a crime you didn't commit.*
> ~Eli Khamarov

Wrap-Up

Which of these beliefs do you hold? Can you see the link between a person's beliefs, actions, and the quality of his life? If we believe we are powerless to create a better life for ourselves and others, what are the likely consequences? If you believe wars and poverty are inevitable and there's nothing you can do, where does that lead? And, if this is the predominant belief of the majority of the population, where does that put us? You guessed it—right where we are now—living in a world of poverty, war, and distress. Is it such a stretch to believe that we need no longer be bound to these antiquated past models of poverty, war, and pain?

Can you look into your heart and believe—really believe— that you, and each and every one of us, deserve a better life? A prosperous, grande life? And that the future will be whatever you envision as possible and probable? With each new empowering belief you choose, a burst of clear energy flows to revitalize your life and begin transforming the fate of our human family. Once our beliefs of prosperity and abundance are solidly formed, emotional energy will trigger those individual and concerted actions needed for change. Those of us already blessed with a grande life shall reap even greater treasures as we help our less fortunate sisters and brothers.

Chapter Nine

Eject Beliefs Harmful to Better Communication and Understanding

You can't not communicate. Everything you say and do or don't say and don't do sends a message to others.
~John Woods

If we are to move beyond a world and people divided by distrust, suspicion, and misunderstanding, it is imperative that we learn how better to communicate and cooperate with one other. Good communication starts at home, and sound principles of communication are the same whether used by individuals, groups, or nations. At the foundation of healthy communication are the core beliefs we hold about ourselves and others. If we believe that we are superior to another because we have more education, expertise, good looks, power, or what have you, this will enter into our interpersonal relationships. Superiority-inferiority dynamics breed contempt, resentment, and ill will. Little can be accomplished in such an atmosphere.

Persons with low self-esteem (flawed beliefs about themselves) have an especially difficult time communicating effectively. To make themselves feel better, they often attempt to put the other person down a notch. An ethnic group or nation with a low self-image acts similarly. Without healthy beliefs about oneself and others, good communication is nigh impossible.

Fundamental tenets for good communication between two individuals or two nations are mutual respect, a willingness to learn from differences, and a nonjudgmental stance. These are born out of a solid belief in oneself and humanity in spite of the quirks and astonishing behaviors we frequently find among members of the human race.

Belief Barriers damaging to communication and understanding often evolve around misconceptions about where our priorities lie, how learning takes place, Western superiority, insensitivity to how our behaviors impact others, and ingrained cultural biases. Five barriers I hear proclaimed over and over are listed below.

Belief Barrier #1

- They're to blame!

    "If my (spouse, boss, kids, government) would just shape up, everything would be fine."

Empowering Belief:

Your power lies in making choices and changes in your own life. Blaming others serves no useful purpose. Everyone is at a different stage of development and understanding. And everyone holds beliefs according to his cultural conditioning and experiences. Attitudes and actions follow accordingly.

Spiritually and psychologically, many of us are crippled. You wouldn't blame someone suffering from a physical handicap and using crutches if he couldn't walk. Fully coming to terms with this in our own minds helps us to be less judgmental and upset, and, in turn, communicate more effectively with others. When you change, others change.

> *Changes in your own life can be the most powerful transformational force in others.*
> ~Juanita Louise Vance

Belief Barrier #2
- **I don't need to be kind to her after the way she acted.**
    "It's payback time!"

Empowering Belief:
No, you don't, and you always have that choice. Keep in mind, however, that how you respond to another's indiscretions and bad behaviors makes more of a statement about you than it does about her. Are your reactions to others following from your core values and who you are? Do you want to revisit your choices here?

> *You can accomplish by kindness what you cannot do by force.*
> ~Publilius Syrus

Belief Barrier #3
- **Family and community first!**
    "My family and community come first. I don't see the value of supporting, or communicating with, people in other countries."

Empowering Belief:
Absolutely correct! Family and community should come first, just as taking care of yourself first is essential if you are to help others. Making choices that support global needs, or communicating with those in other cultures, however, needn't preclude putting your family or community first.

Many people enjoy sharing experiences, or having a friendship link in a different country when visiting on vacation or to discuss humanitarian projects of interest. Vacation traveling with groups of people from other cultures is another way to become acquainted, make friends, and be exposed to new ideas.

On the other hand, perhaps connecting with a person in another culture is not your thing. Prior to taking any action, you need to consider it in light of your values and interests. In the interdependent world we share, however, we need to remember that our attitudes, choices, and actions have far-reaching consequences not only for lives around the globe, but also for our families and home communities.

> *In the progress of personality, first comes a declaration of independence, then a recognition of interdependence.*
> *~Henry Van Dyke*

Belief Barrier #4

- **Assumptions of ignorance about people in Third World countries and among lower socioeconomic status (SES) members of society**

    "I don't believe there is anything to learn from 'those people.'"

Empowering Belief:

Each person has something valuable to contribute to our learning and understanding... irrespective of their formal education or SES status.

Though most of us probably wouldn't admit to having any such Belief Barrier, our actions as Western travelers in other countries would attest to the prevalence of this very misguided belief. Many of us (and I've been guilty, too) on our vacations to other countries take planned spectator tours, go to tourist attractions where we see mostly other Western tourists, stay in Western hotels, and rarely come in contact with the local people.

Eject Beliefs Harmful to Better Communication and Understanding

It is surprising what you can learn by wandering off the beaten tourist track and talking with "common folk." Taking time to chat with taxi drivers, tour guides, maids, homeless (yes, the homeless!), waiters, and clerks during vacation, or anytime, is a marvelous opportunity. If done in a spirit of mutual respect, you'll be pleasantly surprised at the intelligence and insights of "ordinary" people. We can all learn a great deal from each other, and, if even a fraction of the millions of Westerners traveling around the globe on vacation every year became a bit other-centered and made a conscious effort to show kindness, consideration, and appreciation to those they meet, it would surely go a long way toward improving intercultural understanding.

> *The true measure of an individual is how he treats a person who can do him absolutely no good.*
> ~Ann Landers (Esther Friedman Lederer)

Belief Barrier #5
- **Superiority of Western culture and disdain for those who hold different worldviews, have different lifestyles, or different appearances**
  "We're better than you."

Empowering Belief:
We are all part of the human family and deserve to be treated with dignity and respect. In a democracy, no one would quarrel with this statement; however, in practice, it can be a different matter. In Western society, yardsticks for measuring a culture's superiority have primarily been linked to science and technological advances, economic growth, health, and education.

I would argue that the superiority-inferiority dichotomy is not a useful concept, and even harmful for the personal-global goal of good communication and understanding. A more viable measure would be in terms of a culture's beliefs and practices: in what ways do a culture's beliefs benefit or undermine the well-being and happiness of the people? It is, after all, a culture's beliefs that determine their practices and behaviors.

Beliefs that have not served world populations well over the years are those concerning male supremacy, slavery, witchcraft, and revenge. Injudicious beliefs and practices about parenting, punishment, health, nutrition, human sacrifice, infanticide, rape, and the environment—to mention but a few—have proven harmful to members of the human family, and many still threaten our very survival.

Harmful beliefs can be found in most all societies, whether labeled Western, primitive, modern, Third World, or anything else. Identifying those beliefs that are detrimental to the human family is a prerequisite for positive change. Using our personal and media influence to educate, dispel, and replace these beliefs with more empowering beliefs and practices will enrich human lives and move us toward a kinder world of compassion and cooperation.

> *We are still conditioning people in this country and, indeed, all over the globe to the myth of white superiority. We are constantly being told that we don't have racism in this country anymore, but most of the people who are saying that are white. White people think it isn't happening because it isn't happening to them.*
> *-Jane Elliot*

Chapter Ten

Purge Toxic Beliefs That Impede Educational Ideals

> *We are now at the point where we must educate our children in what no one knew yesterday, and prepare our schools for what no one knows yet.*
> ~Margaret Mead

Education is paramount to creating a healthier, more empowered world. A research review by Hannum and Buchmann provides clear evidence that "increased primary and secondary education is associated with improved health, greater economic opportunity, and lower population growth." [1] Children who have completed grade school are "less than half as likely to contract HIV as those without an education."[2] Universal primary education is one of the best weapons against the thousands of people who suffer and die from AIDS each year.[3]

Educational opportunities for each member of society are imperative for the demise of global distress and dysfunction. More than half the adult population cannot read or write, with women accounting for approximately two-thirds of the world's 876 million "illiterates."[4] This is unacceptable, and everyone's responsibility is to bring about change. Indeed, "The total wealth of the world's three richest individuals is greater than the combined gross domestic product . . . of the 48 poorest countries—a quarter of all the world's states."[5]

A host of Belief Barriers thwart our mission for a sound global education for all citizens. Misconceptions about human nature, the dynamics of learning, our roles and responsibilities in the educational process, and false good-evil dichotomies prevent us from developing constructive educational policies, improved curricula, and creative, systemic, action programs.

Three core Belief Barriers permeating much of our thinking and behavior are discussed below. While some of these ideas may challenge your current belief system, I ask you to refrain from judgment, keeping an open mind to new possibilities. When faced with a lack of solid evidence and conflicting or confusing facts on a particular issue, strive to consciously choose those beliefs prompting outcomes in accord with the greater good.

Remember our beliefs and thinking habits determine our decisions and actions. Ultimately, they reflect the world in which we live. All the information isn't in and never will be. We must make choices daily based on partial information. The best strategy is to adopt beliefs and thoughts linked to the consequences we desire. When faced with a choice between two competing belief systems, take a long hard look at where each is likely to lead.

Belief Barrier #1

- **Bad genes**

    "Some people are just bad seeds, and born bad. There's no way we can effectively rehabilitate or change them."

Empowering Belief:

People are born basically good, and how they turn out is a matter of education, learning, and cultural conditioning. Early education is of primary importance.

No one is born with hatred, malice, or prejudice in their heart. We acquire our beliefs, opinions, and ways of thinking from our culture, family, religion, education, and the sum total of our experiences. Many forces act to shape our decisions and actions. The good news is, that with the appropriate instruction and thought tools, we can learn to step back from any faulty belief baggage that is perpetuating the existence of unrest, suspicion, distrust, and inequity in the world today.

Anything that is learned can be unlearned. While this is true at any stage of our development, the earlier we can instill the qualities of stranger-kindness, compassion, creative thinking, and love into the hearts and minds of every child on this planet, the stronger our world will become—and the less vulnerable it will be to poverty, social injustices, suffering, and abuse.

How can we achieve this? Many individuals and organizations are already dedicated in work toward this ambitious ideal. If we make use of current technology through the media, internet, educational institutions, and inspired literature, the possibilities for positive change are phenomenal. Still needed, however, is the collective awareness and support of global citizens throughout the world.

> *In spite of everything, I still believe that people are really good at heart.*
> –Anne Frank

Belief Barrier #2
- Let the experts do it.

    "I'm no authority on global education and what needs to be done to make improvements. Let the experts handle it."

Empowering Belief:
We cannot always rely on "authorities" or "experts" to make the right decisions. Each of us must assume responsibility for those things we cherish, such as education and the well-being of humanity.

Our choices are only as good as the quality of our thinking (or lack thereof) and our mental storehouse of solid information. That said, after researching the data pertinent to our major decisions, and acquainting ourselves with the knowledge of those specializing in a target area, we need to go within our own minds and hearts to arrive at the best decisions.

We live in a society of specialization, and, with the profusion of information, no one—expert or not—can possibly know everything, even within one field of knowledge, much less in other areas. All too often, however, we abdicate our judgment to "the experts." As global citizens, this can get us into lots of trouble. When you let go of your own sense of right and wrong or justice and injustice because you believe "they" know better by virtue of their superior education, position, credentials, or power, you put at risk your integrity, your spiritual well-being, and even your physical and mental health. Others also suffer if we fail to heed our inner voices.

March to the beat of your own drum. At the same time, train yourself to stand free of biases and prejudices picked up in past encounters. Most all decisions must be made without all the facts and with some degree of uncertainty. As best you can, consider the consequences of different beliefs on yourself and humanity; then make a conscious choice to adopt those best for all concerned. Build your bank of beliefs based on solid information and with an awareness of the connection between beliefs and actions; then go inward to that clear space between your beliefs to make the big decisions in your life.

> *Always listen to experts. They'll tell you
> what can't be done and why. Then do it.*
> *~ Robert Heinlein*

Belief Barrier #3
- **Good guys and bad guys**
   "There will always be the 'good guys' and the 'bad guys.'"

Empowering Belief:
Again, how we turn out is a function of our history of past experiences, our culture, and our social conditioning. This, along with our acquired beliefs and thinking habits, makes us who we are today. Changing our collective consciousness with new visions and life-plots can transform the old destructive good-bad dichotomies.

A pervasive theme in our society is of the villains and saints, good and bad persons, and good and evil nations. Children's books, fables from early education, television cartoons, art and video games, portray life as a conflict between the good guys and bad guys. From our toddler years into childhood, adolescence, and adulthood, we are exposed to entertainment and news media that depict life as a nonstop battleground of good and evil forces. Is it any wonder that we believe this is the case? And that it will always be so?

This belief is so strongly embedded in our culture, our thinking, and our way of life, and has built up so much momentum in our entertainment and news media, it seems nigh impossible to imagine anything different. Do we have any chance of coming up with a vision freed from the constant negative imagery we're exposed to?

As a starting point, perhaps we should ask, What would our stories, movies, and fables be, without the conflict between the good guys and bad guys? What kind of society and world would we have, void of the drama of evil and good forces? A boring utopia? Or is there another way of thinking, about a life that offers new dramas, new roles, and brighter visions, all arising from a nonviolent setting? One that leaves behind the villainizing, blaming, prejudice, and the anger, hatred, and animosity of the old dysfunctional good-evil dichotomous world? Really, aren't we just a wee bit tired of this dreary plot?

Only when we learn to break through the hard crust of our mind's long history of conditioning, and reach into the depths of our being for new visions and understandings, will we loosen and dissolve the grip of these destructive paradigms. Educating our young people through stories, media, and games that show new characterizations, role models, and dramas will be a start in this direction.

Collectively, we must strive for a vision that brings us role models showing a better way of life—one based on cooperation and compassion, kindness and trust, prosperity and abundance. As more of these models are created by artists and writers, and become woven into the fabric of our society via the internet, television, and games, we will leave behind the cowboy mentality, the good and bad guys, to enter a stage of living with bountiful creative challenges, yet free from the inhumanity, unnecessary wars, and suffering we see today.

*No one has yet fully realized the wealth of
sympathy, kindness and generosity hidden in the
soul of a child. The effort of every true education
should be to unlock that treasure.*
~Emma Goldman

*Let us think of education as the means of developing
our greatest abilities, because in each of us there is a private
hope and dream which, fulfilled, can be translated into benefit
for everyone and greater strength for our nation.*
~John F. Kennedy

Part IV

CHARGE UP BELIEFS AND MIND BOOSTERS TO POWER YOUR DREAMS

*"The starting point for a better world
is the belief that it's possible.
~Norman Cousins"*

Chapter Eleven

Build a Belief Bank That Empowers Your Life and World!

The thing always happens that you really believe in; and the belief in a thing makes it happen.
~ Frank Lloyd Wright

Your Bank of Beliefs

Our mind is much like a computer and can only run with the beliefs and thoughts about ourselves and life that we have stored there. The only way to break the connection to the old stockpile of defeating beliefs and thoughts is to build a new one. Except when we intervene to make a deliberate decision, 90 percent of the time our minds are pretty much running on autopilot.

As we each make the conscious choice to build upon our mind's vault of empowering beliefs, and begin displacing the destructive remnants of those acquired inadvertently from past conditioning, we will together multiply the global reservoir of mighty beliefs that will move us away from poverty, wars, pain, and suffering. In unison, we will move toward a world of prosperity, social-economic justice, compassion, and kindness.

I have listed below eight core personal-global beliefs at the heart of a better life and world. In building your bank of empowering beliefs, you want to dwell on and play around with the new ideas, i.e., find reasons why they make sense for you to adopt, and the difference they will make in your life and the lives of others.

Core Belief #1—"Believe in yourself!"
- **A solid belief in yourself and your capabilities**

One of the most important beliefs to hold is a solid belief in yourself and your capabilities—to know that you have the power to influence events. If, at a gut level, you believe life is a crapshoot, that it's mostly up to chance and fate, and that what you do doesn't really make much difference, you're not going to have the drive to get out there and make things happen, or to sustain you when things go wrong. When Murphy's Law strikes, and everything goes wrong at the least opportune time, you won't have the inner strength to keep going.

Without a deeply held belief in yourself, you're easy prey to the many temptations, distractions, and daily interruptions that crowd your days. Without a heartfelt belief and trust in yourself and your ideals, you're prone to doubts, discouragement, and disappointment. Decide now to trust your powers to influence change.

> *Man is made by his belief. As he believes, so he is.*
> *~ Bhagavad Gita*

"Believe in others!"
Focus on the best in others. A corollary to believing in yourself is a firm belief in others and their capabilities, irrespective of differences. Living

and working together in a world of richly diverse cultures mandates cooperative, supportive efforts in our quest to create a better world.

> *Believe the best of everybody.*
> ~Rudyard Kipling

> *We are all angels with only one wing.*
> *We can only fly while embracing each other.*
> ~Luciano de Crescenzo

Core Belief #2—"Your choices make a difference!"
- **Your decisions and actions matter**

Your decisions and actions matter—regardless of the outcomes. Even when everything goes wrong and you fail to get the result you want, your efforts and perseverance make a difference.

A common tendency is to become impatient and frustrated when our efforts are thwarted and we don't get the desired outcome. Individually, this has happened to all of us, whether we didn't get the job, the promotion, the relationship, or the championship. You may have worked within a humanitarian organization or corporation seeking to effect positive change, and become discouraged when your efforts seemed to be having little impact. You need to understand that, even though your hard work and efforts may not yet show tangible, physical evidence of change, everything you do with right intention and a good heart is ultimately creating beneficial change at some level.

When you act from the spirit of kindness and service in the best interests of others, your efforts never go unheeded in the larger picture of life. Remind yourself often that, while you do not always have control over the outcome of your actions, you always have dominion over your mind's power to choose and respond.

Every calamity that befalls humanity—whether personal, national, or global—can be turned into an opportunity for creating positive change. We are but a small part of the whole landscape of life, yet we embody and influence each element of the whole. Know that your life and your choices and actions do make a difference, irrespective of any temporary setbacks, apparent failures, or unwanted results. Pat yourself on the back for having the courage to make the effort and take a risk, regardless of how it turns out.

I urge you to continue to persevere in the service of yourself and your world community even during those difficult times when you are discouraged or cannot see any evidence of progress.

> *Life is a place of service, and in that service one has to suffer a great deal that is hard to bear, but more often to experience a great deal of joy. But that joy can be real only if people look upon their lives as a service and have a definite object in life outside themselves and their personal happiness.*
> *~ Count Leo Tolstoy*

Core Belief #3—"Everyone deserves prosperity."

- **Each of us as part of the human family deserves prosperity and a better world**

Another essential belief is a deep conviction that you, and each person, are deserving of prosperity and a better world. Change starts with acceptance, of yourself, as well as others—acceptance and forgiveness for any past mistakes or shortcomings. If, at a deep subconscious level, you don't believe you or others deserve prosperity, socioeconomic justice, and equitable rights, one of two consequences is likely:

1. You'll get right on the verge of achieving an important goal, and then do something to sabotage it.

2. You'll achieve some measure of success in your endeavors, but it will be short-lived, and you'll be unable to sustain it.

In short, you need to believe your efforts will tip fate in humanity's favor, and that *you* are an important determining factor. As greater numbers of people adopt this belief—feel it is so in their hearts and minds—and keep their vision before them, the sooner it will become a reality in our lives and world.

> *Every day, people settle for less than they deserve.*
> *They are only partially living or at best living a partial life.*
> *Every human being has the potential for greatness.*
> *~Bo Bennett*

Core Belief #4—"The world needs your care and compassion."

- **Every corner of the world is affected by policies and practices around the globe. We are all interconnected, and responsible for the welfare of one another.**

This may well be one of the most important beliefs for changing the fate of the world, and moving us past violence, social injustices, and suffering. Violating one person's rights or inflicting pain on another is an insult and injury to our whole human family.

With this concept central to our lives, we embrace a larger vision of compassion and kindness that allows us to reach beyond our differences, and connect with the hearts of others. As this belief becomes an automatic part of our thinking and habits, we will rise beyond fear, abusive conflicts, and insecurity.

Each of us is part of a greater whole and a greater good. Together we can end the divisive global tensions, warfare, and human-inflicted suffering.

As this belief becomes a predominant global view, we will put into practice common goals supportive of all humanity, not just the vested interests of a few.

> *Humankind has not woven the web of life. We are but one thread within it. Whatever we do to the web, we do to ourselves. All things are bound together. All things connect.*
> *~ Chief Seattle*

Core Belief #5—"You are a social being."

- Maintaining a personal-global stance is in the best interests of all humanity

There is some confusion about the democratic ideological position of individualism, that acting in your own self-interest promotes the best interest of others. I see this as a semantic misunderstanding. We are social beings, and, as such, cannot separate out our interests and well-being from those of others. What we do affects others and vice versa, and certainly not necessarily for the better. Seeing the world through global eyes with a view toward the best interests of all humanity is mandatory if we are to learn how to live together in harmony.

Even scientists have recently proven wrong a core theory of classical economics—that human beings are innately selfish and act to maximize their self-interest. New biological research on the hormone oxytocin suggests that we need the mutual support of one another for our very survival.[1]

> *Like the body that is made up of different limbs and organs, all moral creatures must depend on each other to exist.*
> *~ Hindu Proverb*

Core Belief #6—"You can take charge of your beliefs and life."

- Beliefs are tools of the mind, not who you are

Many, many wars have been fought as a result of a nation's beliefs. And many, many individual acts of aggression based on personal beliefs continue to plague our families and world community. In the United States alone, domestic violence accounts for an estimated 5.9 million physical assaults against women annually.[2] And, in the world today, more than sixty million women are "missing" as a result of female infanticide and sex-selective abortions.[3] Capital punishment, though banned in most countries, continues in China, Iran, Israel, and the United States.

All these acts of violence can be traced back to beliefs. Beliefs trigger strong emotions. And beliefs are tied to our identities and how we see ourselves—as strong and powerful, or weak. If we believe that aggressive acts are a sign of strength, and we see ourselves as a strong person or a strong nation, the ill-advised actions are inevitable.

We need fully to understand and appreciate the sweeping implications of the beliefs men and women hold. While heredity plays a role in our temperaments and predispositions, there is no evidence that genes determine our beliefs and thoughts. Indeed, current research by cell biologist Dr. Bruce Lipton suggests the reverse is true—powerful beliefs can change our cells and biology.[4] Until we better grasp how beliefs are formed and how the mind influences behavior, we have little hope for communicating effectively with those who hold opposing views—and for realizing that, given the same conditions (family, education, and culture), we too would share those very same beliefs. Understanding the basics of belief-action dynamics holds enormous promise for positive personal-global influence and change.

> *We can believe what we choose.*
> *We are answerable for what we choose to believe.*
> ~Cardinal John Henry Newman

> *It is not our genes but our beliefs that control our lives.*
> ~Bruce Lipton

> *Beliefs have the power to create and to destroy . . .*
> ~Anthony Robbins

Core Belief #7—"Peace is not won by war."

- **Positive and permanent change is best achieved through peaceful means**

Volumes have been written on this topic. Basically, the position of creating change through peaceful means rests on the assumption that it is not only morally wrong to harm another, with few exceptions, but loaded with unwanted consequences for the perpetrator as well. The deeper sources of aggressive acts, whether at an individual or international level, lie in the discontent and frustration germane to conditions of poverty, social injustice, abuse, and lack of opportunities for creative expression and self-fulfillment.

When we get our priorities straight and have comprehensive action plans to improve effectively these unnecessary conditions, the world will move toward a greater state of peace, cooperation, and trust. For such a momentous change to occur, the first need is to believe genuinely that it is possible. Until we have the solid belief in ourselves to collectively create these conditions and eradicate the poverty and injustice blemishing our world today, we are destined to fail. Positive change follows first from a deep conviction that it is a real possibility. From this stance, a vision begins to take shape which empowers us to take those action steps necessary for the creation of our better world.

Remember too that change starts with you. You are a microcosm of the world. *Be* the world as you would like it to be. Treat others as you would like others to treat you. Gossip, put-downs, insults, racial slurs are all acts of violence. You are the world. Be a better world, and you will see a better world.

> *Ultimately, we have just one moral duty: to reclaim large areas of peace in ourselves, more and more peace, and to reflect it toward others. And the more peace there is in us, the more peace there will be in our troubled world.*
> ~Etty Hillesum

Core Belief #8—"You are more than your beliefs."

- **You have an inner strength and power that exceeds your personal ego power**

Each of us has an inner realm of true strength and power that we can tap into when we let go of our conditioned beliefs and identity. Within this spiritual realm, there is no fear, hatred, anger, malice, or divisive conflict. As more of us learn to access this inner power, our collective spirit of goodwill expands, and a brighter light of hope and love touches the world.

Ideally, your mind's reservoir of beliefs, thinking habits, and thoughts that trigger behavior, is in alignment with this inner force. As you go about your daily routine, making decisions and choices, allow yourself occasional "pause moments" to assess the tone and direction of your life. Is it in tune with the harmony and visions of your true self?

> *Tapping into the solace of your inner self, you experience the calm, clear, pure world of being.*
> ~Juanita Louise Vance

In the next chapter, you'll learn how to capture fully your new, empowering beliefs, and make them a natural part of your daily living.

Chapter Twelve

Give Yourself an Edge with Belief Boosters!

The work of the individual still remains the spark that moves [humankind] forward.
~Igor Sikorsky

Break Out of Flawed Beliefs Permanently!

Belief Boosters are the building blocks of beliefs—supporting thoughts and thinking patterns that answer the question of *why*. Why should I care about a stranger thousands of miles away? Why should I make choices within a global context? Why should I contribute to a better world? Why does what I do matter?

When you ask these power questions, your mind will automatically begin scanning your memory to come up with reasons why. You might hear your inner voice saying, "I'd really like to know that I've done my part to make a difference in the world. I'd like to think that I've made whatever effort I possibly can to end world hunger, suffering, and injustice.

I certainly want to do my best to ensure that my children and grandchildren live in a saner, more peaceful world."

Each of the beliefs in your mind has a cluster of thoughts attached to them. Your task is to develop a group of ideas for the new empowering beliefs, and then shift your focus to these new arguments when the old limiting beliefs surface. You are, in effect, backing up your new personal-global beliefs with sound logic and facts so that they become an automatic part of your thinking and who you are. Belief Boosters act as "convincers" to your mind.

Cement the new empowering beliefs in your mind!

These convincers help cement new beliefs in your mind so that they become a natural part of your thinking and self-image. The more convincers you can come up with, the better. Stocking your mind with convincers, reasons why, why what you do matters, why you can make a difference, will knock out the old lingering doubts.

I suggest you write your new beliefs down on 3x5 cards and carry them with you as a reminder. Put them in your wallet and purse. Post them on your refrigerator, mirrors and bulletin boards. Put them up in your office and in your car. Program them into your iPod, PDA, or iPhone. Constant exposure to the new beliefs and convincers will accelerate the change process.

Activate your emotions

This mind strategy goes beyond positive thinking. For permanent change to occur, you must be *actively and emotionally engaged* in the process. You are coming up with emotionally charged rebuttals to the old ways of thinking. It thus requires more than just a mindless repetition of affirmations. You are destabilizing the old limiting beliefs.

Over our lifetimes, this is generally a gradual process that occurs below the level of our awareness, based on our experiences and exposure to new ideas. By becoming more cognizant of this process, and consciously intervening, you act as a catalyst to speed up the positive changes. Rather than just being a victim of trial and error, hit-or-miss, erroneous information, you learn to step outside of ego and take charge of what's happening—both in your mind and in your life.

> *Whatever you believe with feeling becomes your reality.*
> *~ Brian Tracy*

Activity No. 7
Take Charge of Your Beliefs and Life Now!

A. Explore any Belief Barriers that are preventing you from taking decisive action toward your dreams and goals. List these in the space below:

_____
_____
_____
_____
_____
_____
_____
_____
_____
_____
_____
_____
_____
_____
_____
_____
_____

B. Now go back and refute them with new, empowering beliefs and convincers. Write these down in the space below. Then, cross out the old beliefs, making a conscious intention to let go of each permanently.

_____
_____
_____
_____
_____
_____
_____
_____
_____
_____
_____
_____
_____
_____
_____
_____
_____

Note: Follow the suggestions provided to displace any limiting beliefs that are standing between you and your personal-global vision. Mindstorm for supporting ideas, backing them up with as many convincers as you can dream up. Play around with your new beliefs until they become an easy part of your thought stream and identity. Once you begin to *feel* them, the change process is well on its way to completion. As you start to own the new beliefs, you automatically will act on them. In Step 5, you'll be given specific actions to reinforce your new beliefs and build a better life and world.

Never underestimate the power of your beliefs! If you were to identify and write down all your beliefs, you would virtually see your life played out in front of you. Similarly for a culture—if all the beliefs of a culture could be known, we could predict its direction, prosperity, and well-being.

Remember, too, that "multiple flawed beliefs" are often the source of the problem. It is for this reason that I've waited until you have a fuller view of the wide range of disempowering beliefs we can hold, before listing actions to take. Once you have built a solid foundation of potent beliefs, you are ready to go forward with an action program. Begin by asking yourself the questions in the chapter ahead.

> *Freedom lies beyond belief; however, it is our thoughts and beliefs that create our daily lives. Mastery is achieved through aligned intention, focus and action—all founded on supportive beliefs. If you want to achieve mastery in any area of your life, release your fears and limiting beliefs.*
> *~Marion Culhane*

Chapter Thirteen

Expand Your Horizons With High-Impact Questions

What we need is " more people who specialize in the impossible.
~ Theodore Roethke

To stay motivated, you need to keep your dream of a better life and world before you as you go about your day-to-day activities. And you need to have a dream and vision that stirs your soul, inspires and gives spark and energy to your life. Questions can be a powerful catalyst for change and motivation. What gift will you give to the world?

Don't shy away from big questions. To get big results, we need to ask ourselves big questions. Big questions can inspire and move us to action. Reflect on the questions below as if you are the changing force that will make them a reality. Try to think outside of the typical conditioned boundaries that tell us what we are and aren't capable of doing. In the next chapter, you'll be given specific actions you can take to begin creating a better life and world.

Ask Yourself:

- What if I had the power to end world poverty?
- What if I could be instrumental in changing the fate of a community's homeless?
- What if I could reduce the needless prejudices bringing so much heartache to our society?
- What if I had the power to break the cycle of senseless wars that has destroyed and brought sorrow to so many lives?
- What if I could meet the mighty challenge of educating our youth in nonviolent choices?
- What if I could convince my community leaders to "go green" and impact the global warming threatening the demise of our world?
- What if I could lift humanity out of the dysfunctional conditioned ways that are blemishing our lives?
- What if I could educate and influence the inventors of toys, videos, and games for our youth, so they would produce more products that are fun and challenging but void of aggression and violence?
- What if I could inspire political leaders to explore more promising and peaceful strategies?
- What if I could replace destructive tendencies among youth gangs with creative opportunities?
- What if I had the power to . . . be amazing?!!!

The happy news is: *you do!* You have the power, and you are the hope for our bruised, yet beautiful world. As more and more of us begin taking on personal responsibility for the heartbreaking, unnecessary conditions that plague society, the sooner positive change will come.

> *You must do the thing you think you cannot do.*
> *~ Eleanor Roosevelt*

Five High-Impact Questions for Building a Better World Community

Begin each day with one or more of these questions:

1. How can I best serve others today?

2. What miracle can I create in my life and the lives of others today?

3. What acts of kindness and compassion can I perform today?

4. How can I better move toward a "life of significance" and "prosperity for all"?

5. How might I empower another person's life today?

Questions such as these will help keep you focused and empowered as a global citizen. Your own life will be lifted to a new level of prosperity and happiness.

> *When you are inspired by some great purpose, some extraordinary project, all your thoughts break their bonds; your mind transcends limitations; your consciousness expands in every direction; and you find yourself in a great new and wonderful world. Dormant forces, faculties and talents become alive and you discover yourself to be a greater person by far than you ever dreamed yourself to be.*
> *~ Patanjali*

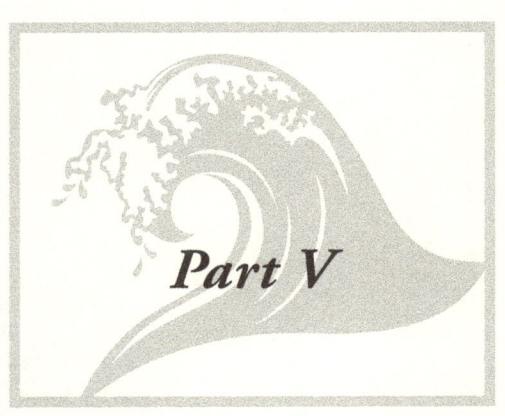

Part V

PUT YOUR DREAMS INTO ACTION!
ACTIONS FOR A BETTER
LIFE AND WORLD
STEP 5

*An idea not coupled with action will never
get any bigger than the brain cell it occupied.*
~Arnold Glasow

*It isn't enough to talk about peace. One must believe in it.
And it isn't enough to believe in it. One must work at it.*
~ Eleanor Roosevelt

*The vision must be followed by the venture. It is not
enough to stare up the steps—we must step up the stairs.*
~ Vance Havner

Chapter Fourteen

Develop Mental-Action Habits to Reinforce Your Vision

> *Do or do not. There is no try.*
> *~ Yoda*

Start by developing mental-action habits

In Step 5, you begin realizing your dreams by imprinting the new empowering beliefs and thoughts in your mind through action. A critical tool to bring about permanent change is to imprint the beliefs in your mind through the use of mental-action habits. The old, self-defeating beliefs are lodged deep within you and are not going to disappear magically overnight. You need to practice running the new beliefs and convincers in your mind.

No time? Well, how about while you're preparing dinner, showering, commuting, working out, waiting in line at the grocer's, doctor's, dentist's, or a dozen other times throughout the day when your mind is running on autopilot with thoughts of worry, uncertainty, and discouragement?

As promised, this book is about spending five minutes or less a day to realize your dreams for a better life and world. Actually the book title is a misnomer, if you follow the steps outlined, you should wind up with *more* energy and time in your life!

Take charge of your mind and dwell on the new empowering beliefs then while going about your daily routine. Make a conscious decision to do these mental rehearsals at least three times a day. You might also want to print or memorize the high-impact questions in the previous chapter to keep you motivated and focused.

When doubts creep in about the benefits of doing this (and they definitely will), remind yourself that *what you believe is what you get.* And what the majority of people in the world believe, will determine the kind of world we live in. Generally, it takes thirty to ninety days for a permanent life style change to occur. The greater number of people around the globe who are committed to positive self-global change, the sooner our lives and world will improve for the better.

"Act as if" your dream is a reality

A second part of the imprinting process to stamp permanently the new beliefs into your mind is to "act on" the new beliefs. When we "act as if" something is so, it becomes so. As you act on the new beliefs, they become more fact than fiction, more true than false, more real in your life. At first you're going to meet resistance. Just as when we start a new exercise program, our muscles are tight and stiff, and they resist. The same is true with our mental muscles; they're going, initially, to resist the new empowering beliefs. You need to practice running them in your mind at regular intervals and then reinforce them in action. There is a back-and-forth process among your beliefs, thinking, and actions. We cannot just think our way to a better life and world. We must act.

Some of the actions listed in the chapters ahead can be taken in only a minute. Others will take longer. Many of the actions are things you're already doing, e.g., shopping, reading, banking, and going on vacation. You may want to revisit and, perhaps, change some of your consumer and entertainment choices—*not* add more to your schedule! Decide which are best suited for your lifestyle and situation. An action for each week of the year—over fifty-two actions—along with suggested web sites are provided in the next chapters and in the Resource Directory. These are grouped under Prosperity, Communication, and Education. This is not intended as an exhaustive list, but one that is diverse enough to offer you a variety of choices. As you take action, remember to keep your dream and vision before you.

> *All our philosophy is dry as dust if it is not immediately translated into some act of living service.*
> *~Mohandas Gandhi*

Chapter Fifteen

Take Action for Personal-Global Prosperity

*How wonderful it is that no one need wait a
single moment before starting to improve the world.*
~Anne Frank

Use Your Spare Time to Boost Personal-Global Prosperity

Below are six specific actions for prosperity that you can begin taking immediately. Please refer to the Resource Directory for additional actions and resources. These include e-mail campaigns, smarter shopping, volunteer activities, travel and transportation choices, financial choices, making donations, and gift giving. A word of caution: while you'll want initially to browse the different actions and web sites according to your interests, take care not to get lost in the maze of information available. Keep in mind your personal vision and goals.

If possible, decide on one action to take *this* week. In the next step, you'll be laying out an action program with target dates and a way to track your progress. For now, strengthen your commitment by checking off at least one action that especially appeals to you, and is in accord with your values and interests.

While many of the suggested actions may appear small or inconsequential, I urge you not to underestimate the power of small steps in your quest for a better life and world. Every tiny action you take in the direction of a more prosperous world, generates energy toward change. Remind yourself as you follow through on these simple actions, that some of the most momentous changes in the world have started with little steps. Dream big, keep a clear vision of the world you desire, and then take the specific and concrete action steps to create it. With each small act, your life, too, will become empowered and enriched.

Help Others to Help Themselves

Action #1:
E-mail and letter-writing campaigns

Subscribe to one of the many organizations that act to persuade Congress to implement programs that get at the root causes of hunger and poverty. For example, instead of giving direct aid to poverty-stricken countries, many organizations help pass legislation that will free money for Third World community development, and provide training in basic job skills, farming, health, and nutrition. Instead of your hard-earned money going to corrupt governments, you are helping people to help themselves. Two organizations which have had impressive results are listed below.

- **Food First Institute for Food and Development Policy**
  This is a nonprofit peoples' think tank and education-for-action center supported by members.
  www.foodfirst.org

- **Bread for the World**
  Bread for the World is comprised of citizens who lobby our nation's decision makers, seeking justice for the world's hungry.
  www.bread.org

Shop for a Better World

Action #2:
Purchase food, clothing, books, and other items through a shopping service that will donate a portion of the purchase price to humanitarian organizations.

- **Shop For Change**
  Buy merchandise through Shop For Change, and a percentage of the purchase price will be donated to progressive organizations such as Educators for Social Responsibility, Alliance for Responsible Trade, National Center for Science Education, Amnesty International, and Physicians for Social Responsibility.

  You can purchase books, organic coffee, music, clothing, and much more from over one hundred online stores, at no extra cost to you.

  Each time you purchase merchandise from one of the retailers on this site, Shop for Change will donate up to 5 percent of the purchase price to progressive causes. Retailers include Barnes & Noble, Lands' End, Gaiam.com, Gardener's Supply Company, Uncommon Goods, and others.
  http://www.credoaction.com

Initially, I recommend that you shop only for a few products—e.g., coffee, tea, or cosmetics—so as not to become discouraged trying to change a lot of your buying habits too quickly.

Keep Our Environment Healthy

Action #3:

On your next road vacation trip, rent a car from the eco-friendly travel club listed below, which sends 1 percent of its annual revenues to environmental clean-up efforts. You will also receive a discount on hybrid car rentals. Other services include emergency roadside assistance, auto/home insurance, and trip planning.

- **Better World Club**
  www.betterworldclub.com

Eat to Save the Earth and Improve Your Health

Action #4:

Eat to save the earth and improve your health.

By increasing your diet of organic vegetables and fruits, you not only lower your risk of atherosclerotic heart disease and breast and colon cancer, but you will also aid prevention of water pollution. Water pollution from such things as pesticides, fertilizer, and manure contaminates more rivers and streams than do all the wastes from United States industries and cities combined. See web site below for more information.

- **International Vegetarian Union**
  http://www.ivu.org/

Sustain Global Prosperity Through Your Financial Institutions

Action #5:

Invest in SRIs (Socially Responsible Investments)

Align your financial goals with your personal values by investing in socially responsible money market funds. Typical social screens used are Weapons/Defense, Gambling, Liquor, Tobacco, Nuclear Power, Fair Hiring Policies and Practices, Environmental Responsibility, Products/Services that enhance the quality of life, and International Development.

How do SRIs perform? Many have outperformed nonSRIs. Overall, in the last decade, SRIs have returned an average 9.1 percent a year, compared with 9.4 percent average for all U.S. stock funds.[1] Others have performed significantly better. The United Nations has recently officially endorsed SRIs as the international standard. Choose from over one hundred SRIs. Several of these funds with different screens are listed below.

- **Winslow Green** serves high-net-worth individual investors and institutions by investing in environmentally conscious companies. They have been doing "green" investing since 1983.
  www.winslowgreen.com

- **Pax World Women's Equity Fund** invests in forward-thinking companies. It also seeks to advance equality, promote peace, and protect the environment.
  http://www.paxworld.com/funds/womens-equity-fund

- **Amana Funds** makes investments in companies that adhere to Islamic principles.
  www.amanafunds.com

- **Pax World's Funds** have a $250 minimum initial investment. Choose from Balanced Funds, Growth Funds, and High Yield Funds, among others.
  www.paxworld.com

- **The Calvert Group** selects socially and environmentally conscious mutual funds.
  http://www.calvertgroup.com/

Need more information, or help selecting SRI funds? Check out these two web sites:

- **Social Funds** is a comprehensive personal finance web site with reports, statistics, performance ratings, and news on a variety of socially responsible investments.
  http://preview.tinyurl.com/cefvrn

- **Natural Investments LLC (NI)**
  NI pioneered socially responsible investing in the 1980s, and works on a management fee basis. Hal and Jack Brill, founders, are the authors of *Investing From the Heart* and *Investing With Your Values*. See their web site for full information.
  www.naturalinvesting.com

Take Action for Personal-Global Prosperity

Purchase Gifts That Empower People and Protect Our Planet

The gifts you give not only make a statement about your values, but can promote cultural prosperity, helping others to help themselves.

Action #6:

Buy gifts, services, and products from those shops and organizations that are helping others to help themselves. Visit the three web sites below for more information.

- **Ten Thousand Villages**
  Purchase unique, fair-trade, handcrafted gifts made by people around the world. See their web site to find a store in your area. Your purchase makes a difference!
  www.tenthousandvillages.com

- **Alternative Gifts International**
  Buy gifts that empower people in crisis, protect our planet, and build peace. A few examples of alternative gifts you'll find here:
  - Build a School in Afghanistan
  - Help Endangered Girls in Cambodia
  - Buy a Book—Train a Teacher in Haiti
  - Rescue an Orphan in China
  - Solar Water Pumps in Latin America
  - Eye Service for the Poor in Honduras

  Giving a value gift for a birthday, anniversary, or other occasion, will help build a partnership with those in need, and promote global goodwill.
  www.altgifts.org

- **ModestNeeds.Org**

    This organization seeks to stop poverty before it begins by making small emergency loans to those in need, e.g., to help an individual or family who has had a temporary setback due to an illness or unexpected expense. They also contribute to small, worthy, nonprofit organizations. You can support their efforts by shopping at their CafePress store as well as other options.

    http://www.modestneeds.org/

    http://www.cafepress.com/modestneeds/

- **Practical Action (PA)**

    Practical Action is a development charity working with poor people in India, Africa, and Latin America, to help them develop the skills and tools necessary to build a better life. It was founded in 1966 by economist Dr. E. F. Schumacher, based on his philosophy that small changes can make a big difference.

    Help raise money for PA by shopping at Amazon, eBay, or Charity Flowers, or using the Everyclick web site.

    http://practicalaction.org/?id=giveasyoushop

More actions for personal-global prosperity are listed in the Resource Directory.

> *Whatever you do may seem insignificant to you,*
> *but it is most important that you do it.*
> *~ Mahatma Gandhi*

Chapter Sixteen

Act to Build Better Communication and Understanding

*Communication leads to community, that is,
to understanding, intimacy and mutual valuing.*
~Rollo May

Taking one or more of the suggested actions in this chapter will not only help build a more cooperative and compassionate world, but offer you abundant opportunities as well. And, as you reach out to others, don't be surprised if you are rewarded with some deeply satisfying and happy experiences. My clients tell me that their most fulfilling moments have followed from taking actions here.

Giving service gifts and participation in online intercultural forums and cultural exchange programs are just a few of the ways to begin building better intercultural relationships. Join forces with like-minded groups acting to eliminate cultural misconceptions and misunderstandings. Six suggested actions, along with supporting web links, are provided below. After surveying the possibilities, highlight those that resonate with you.

Join an Online Forum for Intercultural Cooperation and Understanding

Action #1:
Exchange information with like-minded people around the world through an online information forum with an aim toward promoting dialogue and international cooperation. See web site below to get started.

- **Mandat International (MI)**
  MI is a nonprofit organization, the mission of which is to promote dialogue and international cooperation. Its web site includes a calendar of international meetings and conventions, information on skills exchange and volunteering, plus over one thousand useful links.
  www.mandint.org

Take a Reality Tour

Action #2:
Take a reality tour with like-minded people and learn firsthand about a country of interest. What breakthroughs have they had in conflict resolution, or putting an end to social and economic injustices? Converse with community leaders and locals. Check the web site below for dates and prices.

- **Global Exchange**
  Meet with community leaders in Ireland, Cuba, Haiti, or South Africa. Talk with locals and participate in community projects.
  www.globalexchange.org/tours

Celebrate Diversity

Action #3:

How much cultural diversity is reflected in your home? Check out the literature, music, crafts, and artwork in your home. Assess what kind of statement you're making when others visit you. Do you want to eliminate anything or add something new?

Volunteer for a Global Service Trip

Action #4:

Volunteer some time to work in another country to help foster friendships and build cultural goodwill. A list of web sites is provided below. Select one that aligns with your values and lifestyle.

- **Habitat for Humanity International**
  An ecumenical Christian organization that helps families in the U.S. and other countries build affordable housing. Volunteer for one- to three-week trips.
  www.habitat.org

- **Global Citizens Network**
  Offers one- to three-week service trips around the world. Be part of a group working on projects initiated by locals in the community. Projects range from teaching business skills to setting up a library or health clinic.
  www.globalcitizens.org

- **Global Volunteers**
  Spend one to three weeks working in countries such as Ireland, India, Australia, or Costa Rica. Volunteer your time in local communities

to teach, provide health care, do environmental work, construction, childcare, or tutoring. No specialized skills are required.
www.globalvolunteers.org

- **Cross-Cultural Solutions**
  An international volunteer organization with programs in such countries as China, Russia, Tanzania, India, and Thailand. Participate in community development projects with local people.
  www.crossculturalsolutions.org

- **Action Without Borders**
  Action Without Borders is independent of any government, or political or religious creed. Learn about events and volunteer opportunities in countries throughout the world, such as Chile and New Zealand. Connect with people around the world who share your interests and goals. Its web site includes a Career Center, Resources for Teachers, Tools for Nonprofit Organizations, Tips for Volunteers, and much more!
  www.idealist.org

Take a Vacation that Promotes Intercultural Understanding

Billions of dollars are spent each year on vacation travel. What impact are your vacation activities having on people in the countries you visit?

Vacations are an excellent time to share information and learn more about another culture. How you spend your time and money on a vacation reflects your values.

Action #5:
Set aside some of your vacation time to visit or stay with locals. Register with one of the international host networks and arrange to share a

Act to Build Better Communication and Understanding

meal or stay at a local home. Experience other cultures more deeply than just as "a tourist." One of these is given below:

- **SERVAS International**
  Visit foreign countries and communicate with people in different cultures on real issues. SERVAS was founded in 1949 and has members in over 130 countries who will welcome you into their homes. Person-to-person contacts can make an important difference in building world peace and understanding. A small annual fee is charged to register with SERVAS.
  www.servas.org

Build Peace and Cooperation in Children through the Gifts You Give

Action #6:
Buy toys, games, books, and music for your children, grandchildren, nieces, and nephews that celebrate cultural diversity and nonviolence. Refuse to buy guns, and games that promote hatred and revenge.

- See Resource Directory for more suggestions on how you can aid global cooperation and understanding.

> *"Life is the first gift,*
> *love is the second,*
> *and understanding the third."*
> *– Marge Piercy*

Chapter Seventeen

Actions for a Sounder and Saner Education

> *Education is for improving the lives of others and for leaving your community and world better than you found it.*
> *~Marian Wright Edelman*

Education matters!

Staying abreast of world events and other cultures through reliable information, positions us better to understand and act on the important issues of society. Playing a role in educating the less fortunate in developing countries about women's rights, democracy, health, and social-economic opportunities, will lessen injustices and acts of aggression, and improve the well-being of all.

A study conducted by International Food Policy Research Institute (IFPRI) found that increases in women's education reduced child malnutrition by 43 percent. Increases in women's status also accounted for a 12 percent reduction in child malnutrition between 1970 and 1995.[1]

Together, increases in women's education and status reduced child malnutrition by more than 50 percent in developing countries.

Hawaii education expert Randy Hitz contends that "investing in the care and education of our young children must be among the highest priorities for any state or nation that seeks to perpetuate a vibrant economy, peace and justice for its citizens."[2]

Listed below are six suggestions for the advancement of personal-global education. Online contact information is provided for each. Get started today by highlighting those actions that align with your personality and interests. See the Resource Directory for additional actions. Remember, small actions can create mighty results!

Stay Informed about Vital Global Issues

Action #1:
Keep yourself and your family informed about global issues with quality books and media. Visit your library, or rent or order books listed in the Resource Directory's Bibliography at the end of this book. You might also want to check out one of the socially responsible publishers listed below, to place an order.

- **Heartsong Books**
  Heartsong is a publisher of books that celebrate the interconnectedness of life. It offers books of inspiration, compassion, and spirit. Its web site also lists multicultural children's books.
  www.heartsongbooks.com

- **New Society Publishers**
  New Society publishes books for fundamental social change through nonviolent action.
  www.newsociety.com

- **Nation Books**
  Nation Books is a progressive publisher with books on the social and cultural forces shaping our lives. Books are available on human rights, art and culture, feminism, race, environment, and much more.
  http://www.nationbooks.org/

Keep Abreast of Human Rights Projects and Get Involved

Action #2:

Subscribe to Amnesty International's Human Rights Education Newsletter and take action in minutes on educational issues of concern. Let your voice be heard!

www.amnesty.org

Promote Health Education and Empowerment in Underdeveloped Countries

Action #3:

Aid health education and empowerment in underdeveloped countries.

If you are interested in health education in underdeveloped countries, you'll want to visit the Hesperian Foundation listed below. They offer a number of ongoing volunteer projects. Read their current newsletter online, and learn about the many activities in which you can become involved.

- **Hesperian Foundation**
  The Hesperian Foundation is a nonprofit publisher of books and newsletters for community-based health care and empowerment. They publish *Where Women Have No Doctor* and *Where There Is No Doctor*, books that have been widely used in underdeveloped, poverty-stricken countries in which the vast majority of people do not have access to medical facilities.
  www.hesperian.org

Help End Illiteracy in Underdeveloped Countries

Action #4:
Make a donation of air miles to help end illiteracy in Central America. A donation of fifty thousand points through American, Continental, Delta, Taca, or United Air Lines for the round-trip will support book deliveries in Central and South American communities. Check out the web site below for detailed information on this and other ways to support the education of elementary children in Central and South America.

- **Books for a Better World (BBW)**
  BBW is an organization designed to end illiteracy in developing countries—a major factor in the dependence of developing countries on foreign financial assistance. Books for a Better World seeks to motivate and empower children in developing countries through establishing libraries and scholarship programs.
  http://www.booksforabetterworld.org

Become Involved in "Conflict Evolution"

Action #5:
Visit the site below and discover how "Conflict Evolution" in theatre and other arts is being successfully used to teach children and youth about peace—within themselves and with others. This is a program based in Ontario, Canada, and its successful techniques are greatly in demand. If you are interested in peace building, this is a site you'll definitely want to check out.
www.childrenspeacetheatre.org

Promote Multicultural Awareness
Via Classroom Global Collaboration

Action #6:

Promote multicultural awareness through international learning teams. The site below is dedicated to promoting multicultural awareness by connecting K-12 classrooms worldwide into international learning teams. Click to discover how you can participate in this project to make the world a better place. Friends and Flags is headquartered in Israel.

- **Global SchoolNet**
  Friends and Flags
  http://www.gsn.org/programs/friendsandflags or
  www.friendsandflags.org

- See Resource Directory for additional suggestions on how you can improve education in our world today.

> *Education is the most powerful weapon*
> *which you can use to change the world.*
> *~Nelson Mandela*

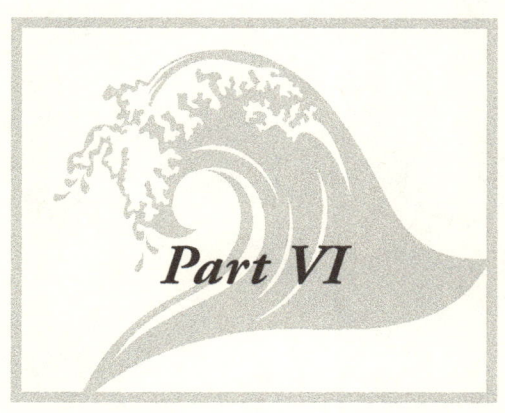

Part VI

STAYING MOTIVATED
KEEPING THE MOMENTUM ALIVE
STEP 6

*" If we did everything we were capable of,
we would astound ourselves.
~ Thomas Edison "*

Chapter Eighteen
STEP 6
Design Your Time Plan: Set Target Dates and Track Your Progress

Wisdom is knowing what to do next; virtue is doing it.
~David Star Jordan

To follow through effectively on the actions you have elected to take for a better life and world, it is important to set target dates and track your progress. For this step, I suggest you use a calendar to enter the target dates for each of the actions you've committed yourself to taking.

For example, say you'd like to broaden your understanding of another culture through a friendship link. When are you going to make the initial contact? With which country will you begin? For a global prosperity goal, perhaps you've decided to change your bank account to a socially responsible bank that invests its dollars in helping low-income communities in Third World countries help themselves. Make a note in your calendar for a specific time and date to follow through. Setting up a credit card which sends a portion of the proceeds from your purchases toward a favorite charity is another action you've been thinking about doing. When? Entering them in your calendar reaffirms your intentions and choices.

You can download a free **Better Life & World Calendar** at http://www.drjan.net/calendar. Or use your own web calendar. Personalize it by jotting down a few of the motivational quotations sprinkled throughout this book. Especially take a look at those in the Resource Directory under "Quotations to Motivate and Prompt Action." Inside your calendar, you'll be entering the dates and texting in the specific actions you have elected to take. Some will be one-time events, such as changing your bank account or investing in SRIs. Others, like volunteering for a human rights organization, may be an hour once every month.

If possible, complete a full year of these better living choices. Once you have them in your calendar, it's easier to follow through. Block the times out in your calendar after reading this chapter. Don't try to be too ambitious and do everything at once. Start small. One to three actions per month is ideal. Consistency is the key.

Even though pursuing many of your goals may be an ongoing process, you need to keep track of your time, and regularly rate yourself on your activities and outcomes. This will boost your confidence in knowing that you are living your values and walking your talk.

If you have explored the diverse range of actions detailed in the last few chapters and the Resource Directory, my guess is you've already taken some actions and are well on the way to creating a better life for yourself and others. Think of each action you take as an "act of greatness." It is! No matter how small or simple the action appears, remember that each step you take is building a better world. Pat yourself on the back, and allow yourself to feel triumphant.

Track Your Progress

Next, decide how you're going to track your progress toward your goals, e.g., monthly, quarterly, semi-annually. At the end of each period, rate your progress on a scale from 1 to 5, with 5 being highest. If you score below 4, reread the section on "Quotations to Motivate and Prompt Action." You might also want to review more of the recommended actions in the Resource Directory. Check those that align with your personal vision and dreams for a better life and world.

To make things even easier, on the next page is a calendar with a recommended action for every month of the year. If you choose to follow this guide, take a few minutes to commit yourself mentally to three actions for the next three months of the year.

> *We cannot seek or attain health, wealth, learning, justice or kindness in general. Action is always specific, concrete, individualized, unique.*
> *~ Benjamin Jowett*

12-Month Calendar of Actions for a Better Life & World

January
- **Positive Beliefs Day** – 1 January
- **Dream a Better World Day** – 1 January

Recommended Action:
Start the year on a positive note!
　Read or order your copy of *Yes! A Journal of Positive Futures* to learn about and support people dedicated to creating a just, sustainable, and compassionate future. You can download a trial issue free.
See the **Positive Futures Network**—www.futurenet.org.

February
- **Freedom Day** – 1 February
- **International Mother Language Day** – 21 February

Recommended Action:
Switch to a long-distance or wireless service that donates a portion of the money you pay for long-distance calls to a human rights organization such as Oxfam Canada and Amnesty International.
See Credo (a program of Working Assets)—www.credomobile.com.

March
- **International Women's Day** – 8 March
- **International Day for the Elimination of Racial Discrimination** – 21 March
- **World Day for Water** – 22 March

Recommended Action:
Join an online women's forum to exchange information and resources with women in other countries. Make new friendships, share ideas, and interests. See Feminist Majority Foundation—www.feminist.org. FMF,

founded in 1987, is dedicated to women's equality, reproductive health, and nonviolence. Through research and action, FMF seeks to empower women economically, socially, and politically.

April
- **World Health Day** – 7 April
- **Earth Day** – 22 April

Recommended Action:

Buy organically grown products for your family's health and for preservation of the environment. Select three products you will purchase this month, e.g., organic coffee, broccoli, and tomatoes.

May
- **World Day for Cultural Diversity** – 21 May

Recommended Action:

Shop online at SERRV International, a nonprofit trade organization that promotes social and economic justice in over forty developing regions throughout the world. SI provides help in developing and marketing local food products and handcrafts.
See www.serrv.org.

June
- **International Day of Innocent Children Victims of Aggression** – 4 June
- **World Environment Day** – 5 June
- **World Refugee Day** – 20 June
- **Interfaith Day** – 22 June

Recommended Action:

Improve your vocabulary and donate rice free through the UN to help end world hunger. http://www.freerice.com

July
- **International Day of Cooperatives** – 7 July

Recommended Action:

This summer, set aside some vacation time to further the aims of improved global communication and understanding. Join forces with a like-minded group acting to eliminate cultural misconceptions and misunderstandings. Spend one to three weeks working in countries such as Ireland, India, Australia, or Costa Rica. Volunteer your time in local communities to teach, provide health care, do environmental work, construction, childcare, or tutoring. No specialized skills are required.
See Global Volunteers—www.globalvolunteers.org.

August
- **International Day of the World's Indigenous People** – 9 August
- **International Youth Day** – 12 August

Recommended Action:

Register with an international host network and arrange to stay at a local home during your vacation. Or invite someone from elsewhere to stay at your home. Meet people from another culture to increase intercultural understanding. Check out SERVAS International—www.servas.org.

September
- **International Literacy Day** – 8 September
- **International Peace Day** – 21 September

Recommended Action:

Apply for a credit card that allots a percentage of the money you spend on purchases, to human rights organizations such as Amnesty International, Human Rights Campaign, and Oxfam Canada. See Citizens Bank Shared Interests VISA— www.citizensbank.ca.

October
- **International End Poverty Day** – 17 October

Recommended Action:

Purchase unique, fair-trade, handcrafted gifts made by people around the world. Visit their web site to find a store in your area. Your purchase makes a difference!
Visit Ten Thousand Villages—www.tenthousandvillages.com.

November
- **World Kindness Day** – 13 November
- **Abundant World Harvest Day** – 16 November

Recommended Action:

Support a micro-lending organization that helps indigenous people to help themselves and their communities by giving them small loans to start a business.
See Kiva—www.kiva.org.

December
- **Human Rights Day** – 10 December
- **International Migrants Day** – 18 December

Recommended Action:

Support the charity of your choice while doing your holiday shopping. The site below allows you to shop at over 400 major retailers and specialty shops throughout the United States, and will return a portion of what you spend to your designated cause.
www.iGive.com

A Brief Checklist for Discretionary Time Choices

While it is recommended that you build your own personal checklist of discretionary time choices and actions, below is a brief guide to some of the actions we've looked at. Review the Resource Directory in Part IX for sources and alternative actions you may want to consider.

- Join an online intercultural forum to share information and ideas.

- Furnish your home according to your values. Do your artwork, furniture, entertainment, music, and games reflect who you are? Does your home celebrate cultural diversity?

- Choose products, clothing, and furnishings made from natural materials.

- Whenever possible, buy products produced locally to support your community and conserve energy.

- Keep it simple. Conspicuous consumption to impress others is not impressing anyone.

- Consider giving "value" gifts on special occasions to friends and family. Help someone less fortunate!

- Buy organically grown products for your family's health and for preservation of the environment.

- Support peaceful living through nonaggressive entertainment choices. Avoid war toys and games.

- Plan your vacations and leisure activities in accord with your personal-global values and goals.

- Treat the environment with reverence and respect in your daily living.

- Read, listen to, and watch media (newspapers, magazines, ezines, television, radio) that give accurate and reliable information about your community and world. Remember, your choices are largely based on the knowledge and information you have received.

Stay Empowered!

- *Express gratitude and appreciation for the many gifts life offers.*

- *Regularly nourish your mind* with inspirational and motivational messages. A nutritious mental and emotional diet keeps your health intact.

- *Be observant of how your mind works:* information plus experiences equal your beliefs. Beliefs produce your emotions and actions. Your experiences, in turn, feed back to form your beliefs. You have the power to intervene through choice.

- *Step free of faulty beliefs* into your "freedom space" to make the big decisions in your life. Regularly weed out lethal beliefs, and replace them with empowering beliefs. Strive to keep your beliefs aligned with the qualities of your soul: kindness, compassion, reverence for life, creativity, and abundance. Know that you are the director of your mind and, therefore, your life. Know that your beliefs, choices, and actions impact the whole body of humanity. Know that you have the power to influence global change in a positive direction. Know that your own health and well-being depend on a healthy universe.

- *Keep your vision* of prosperity for all, peaceful coexistence, and global education. Rehearse and reinforce this vision daily. *Believe* in your power to make it a reality. *Act* to create the world you desire.

Schedule Regular Personal-Global Checkups

Just as we have an annual physical checkup to preserve our health, we need to schedule personal-global well-being checkups. We live in a changing world, and what we've learned to do today for our mutual benefit may be misguided tomorrow. This needn't take much time, and will ensure that you and our world stay in the best possible shape.

Remember: your choices are only as accurate and responsible as the content of your mind. Without regular scrutiny of this content for errors and alignment with your mission in life, you are subject to unwanted consequences. Review and revise your Personal-Global Vision Statement often to ensure that you stay on the path of your particular passion.

Keep your inner network of beliefs and thoughts under the spotlight of an expanded global vision. Manifesting this vision in simple, specific "acts of greatness" will spark new energy into your days. Congratulate yourself frequently for your choice and commitment to make a difference!

As more and more people like yourself begin to see the world through the compassionate lens of our connectedness to each other, songs and celebrations will replace the sadness and suffering. *You* are the catalyst!

You really can change the world if you care enough.
~Marian Wright Eldeman

Chapter Nineteen

Five Minutes a Day Is All It Takes!

Set out each day believing in your dreams. Know without a doubt that you were made for amazing things.
  ~Josh Hinds

Below is a recap of the key ideas we've been discussing to create change using the tools of vision, belief, and action. While you may well wish to spend more than five minutes a day, I wrote this book so that every person—no matter how busy her schedule, work commitments, or obligations—would be able to transform her life and world.

SEE IT!

Visualization is a key component to realizing your dreams for a better life and world. For your dream to manifest, you need to keep it alive in your imagination. To aid this process, I recommend that each morning you text your vision statement on your wireless or laptop. Keep it short; twenty-five words or fewer is perfect. Make it a habit as routine as brushing your teeth in the morning. Consistency is vital to success. Be sure and write your vision statement in the present tense, as if it has already transpired. Stay focused on the desired results of what you want, not what you *don't* want. Remember: what you focus on expands. This cannot be overemphasized. What you give your attention to is what you will receive. Continually refine and focus your dream intention with laser-sharp precision. *See It, Feel It, Be It!*

You're not going to be perfect at this and you don't have to be. If you miss a day or two writing your vision statement, or cannot always see it clearly in your mind's eye, it's okay. Pick up where you left off, but, by all means, continue! I missed writing mine seventeen days last year. Just do your best and I guarantee you'll start seeing results. For more tips and guidelines on visualization, visit http://www.drjan.net/VisionTips.pdf and http://www.drjan.net/VisionGuidelines.pdf. You can download them free.

Spend one to two minutes daily visualizing your dream.

BELIEVE IT!

Believe in your vision. Believe in your powers to make your dream a reality. Your beliefs have the energy to transform your life and the world in which we live. The stronger the belief, the stronger the energy behind it. Believe in yourself and your power to create change. Believe in others. Believe in the universe. Believe in the real possibility and *probability* of abundance for your life and world. You have the power to make it happen! Instead of worrying and fretting over all the things going wrong in your life, choose to dwell on what's going right! Run the new beliefs and thoughts through your mind regularly throughout the day while doing household chores, showering, waiting in lines, exercising, or other activities.

How much time does this take? Nada! You're pumping new beliefs into your mind and dislodging the old ones while going about your normal routine. Plus you'll get a big bonus: *more time and energy!* Like physical exercise, positive mental exercise will give you extra energy and zest. When you fully believe in yourself and the real probability of your dreams coming true, you'll start feeling lighter and more joyful. Use the Belief Boosters in Chapter 12 to cement the empowering beliefs in your mind. Additional mind tools can be found at http://www.drjan.net/bonus.

> *What you think about becomes reality . . .*
> *Think only great thoughts.*
> *~Aretta Swanson*

> *Believing in yourself and what you are doing is*
> *the most important rung on the ladder of success.*
> *~Alan Cohen*

ACT ON IT!

Take action in the direction of your dreams. When you live as a global citizen, your actions will be empowering all humanity. Prosper by helping others prosper. Plan to take one to three of the actions listed in the Resource Directory each month. By now, you've no doubt already begun the transformation process and taken action; however—just in case—to help you reinforce your commitment to change, I've listed below *five no-cost actions you can take in less than three minutes:*

1. E-mail or text something of value to a business acquaintance, colleague, or friend. For example, it could be a helpful web link, ezine article, or a client referral.

2. Sign the ONE Declaration to help fight global AIDS and extreme poverty—http://www.one.org/declare.

3. Post an inspirational message, video, or picture on one of the social media networks, e.g., Facebook, Twitter, or Squidoo.

4. Improve your vocabulary and donate rice free through the UN, to help end world hunger—http://freerice.com.

5. Help build self-worth in a person who is homeless by asking her opinion on a social issue.

Please don't underestimate the value of acting in the service of others. Every time you act in the service of another, you are rewarded twofold. Simple, everyday choices and actions can, and will, transform your life and the life of the world. Live the life you were intended to live. Become a co-creator of the abundance and happiness of people everywhere.

> *Good thoughts are no better than*
> *good dreams, unless they be executed.*
> *~Ralph Waldo Emerson*

> *Let him who would move the world first move himself.*
> *~Socrates*

> *Concerning all acts of initiative and creation,*
> *there's one elementary truth—the moment one*
> *definitely commits oneself, providence moves too.*
> *~Goethe*

Part VII

CONGRATULATE YOURSELF AND CELEBRATE!
STEP 7

" Celebrate what you want to see more of.
~ Thomas J. Peters "

Chapter Twenty
STEP 7
Congratulate Yourself and Reap the Rewards!

*If something comes to life in others because of you,
then you have made an approach to immortality.*
~Norman Cousins

Whatever small action steps you take in the service of humanity build self-empowerment and help move you past doubts, anxieties, and the insecurity of uncertainty. You no longer feel helpless to change the course of events, but have become an active global partner for positive change. Congratulations!

    I have summarized below some of the marvelous benefits resulting from your choice to step up to the plate and bring a better world into being. When you become discouraged, keep this battery of belief-benefit reminders handy to draw upon for inspiration and motivation. Make them a regular part of your daily internal dialogue. During troubling times, we need a solid mental-spiritual platform to keep us going. With your expanded beliefs and empowered thinking habits, nothing will be able to shake you from your mission.

- **Protects Your Mental-Emotional Health**
  When we fail to live our lives in ways that keep our whole body of humanity healthy, we put our personal well-being at risk. An undercurrent of discontent and sadness permeates our lives when we neglect our responsibility to the vital whole of humanity. Stay healthy with global-minded living!

- **Enhances Personal Well-Being and Enrichment**
  Our deeper purpose and meaning in life can only evolve through service to others—whether it takes the form of direct assistance, creative endeavors, communication, education, or other kinds of actions.

  Having a larger perspective that serves humanity expands your consciousness and enriches every dimension of your life. Knowing that you are a partner in the care of the world lifts you past the mundane irritations and annoyances threatening your days. You just plain *feel* better! And when you feel better, you're going to do more for yourself, your community, and world.

- **Spiritual Growth**
  When you act with compassion and courage in the interests of humanity, you grow spiritually.

  Being blessed with having our essential needs of clean water, food, and shelter met, opens the door for opportunities to help meet the needs of those less fortunate. Failing to help others in need erodes our spiritual health. Ignoring our innermost voices strikes at the heart of our souls. Simple "acts of kindness" will change the world, and *you*!

- **It's the Right Thing to Do**
  From a moral stance, it's just plain wrong to allow needless suffering, poverty, and injustices to continue when each of us can do something to bring about positive change. Take whatever small steps you can, and know that you *are* making a difference. No matter how small the light, it shines through the darkness.

- **Safeguards Your Children, Grandchildren, and Future Generations**
  Our very survival as a human race is at stake. Perhaps in times past, we could ignore our responsibilities as global agents for the welfare of humanity. This is no longer true—if ever it was. We live in an interdependent world, and need to adjust our beliefs, thinking, and actions accordingly. Act according to the calling of your soul, and the whole world will be safer and saner.

- **Brings Deep Joy and Meaning into Your Life**
  You wouldn't have the desire to reach out to humanity if it wasn't a possibility and part of your greater purpose. Trust your heartfelt desires to serve humanity. The adventure of meeting better-world challenges will supercharge your life with rich meaning and fulfillment.

What we have done for ourselves alone dies with us; what we have done for others and the world remains and is immortal.
~Albert Pike

Everyone has the power for greatness, not for fame but for greatness, because greatness is determined by service.
~Martin Luther King, Jr.

I don't know what your destiny will be, but one thing I do know: the only ones among you who will be really happy are those who have sought and found how to serve.
~Albert Schweitzer

Part VIII

EPILOGUE

*Everyone should carefully consider
which way his heart draws him, and then
choose that way with all his strength.*
-Hasidic Saying

The Mind-Heart Distinction

> *If we could see the miracle of a single flower clearly,*
> *our whole life would change.*
> *~ Buddha*

As you recall, our actions are triggered by our beliefs, thinking, thoughts, and perceptions. For the bulk of our lifetimes, we're on autopilot according to these beliefs and thinking habits.

Our hearts are a different matter altogether. Responding from our hearts—our pure essences—we're consistently kind, compassionate, and loving. Each and every one of us is at our best in this divine space. By our very nature here, we could not injure or harm another.

In an ideal world, we would all connect to one another and act routinely from our hearts. In the real world, however, we act routinely and automatically from within the mind contexts of our beliefs and reasoning, and the culture built from those beliefs—family, religion, political, military, and socioeconomic systems.

Only when we're able to step back from our own minds' sets of beliefs and past conditioning, do we touch upon the essence of ourselves, and have the awareness to act in accord with our divine spirits. It is out of this clear awareness that we are able to create new forms, structures, and systems that reflect our natural spirits of kindness, compassion, and cooperation.

Practically and realistically, however, humans do not live in this perfect space. Ninety per cent or more of our behavior is automatic, driven by our conditioned selves' current stock of beliefs and thoughts. And our world runs according to the existing socioeconomic and political-military systems built by Jack's mind.

Until we reach that "critical mass" and evolve a new species—as Albert Einstein and other great scientists and spiritual leaders have predicted is in the making—we are largely at the mercy of the ways in which our present intellects, emotions, and society function. By increasing our understanding of belief-social dynamics and their personal-global consequences, however, we can better prepare for the inevitable, prevent possible socioeconomic disasters, and improve many of the conditions of our world community.

Educating ourselves in those empowering beliefs that align with our true nature of goodness, and making a conscious effort to instill them in our lives, will move us in the direction of a better, albeit not perfect, world. And who knows? Perhaps somewhere along the way, before we blow ourselves off the face of the earth, with the right intention and a greater concerted global citizen effort, we'll make that quantum leap in our consciousness, see a qualitative difference, and evolve a miraculous new species.

Epilogue

*A human being is part of the whole
called by us universe . . . We experience ourselves,
our thoughts and feelings as something separate
from the rest—a kind of optical delusion of consciousness.
This delusion is a kind of prison for us, restricting us to
our personal desires and to affection for a few persons
nearest to us. Our task must be to free ourselves from
the prison by widening our circle of compassion to
embrace all living creatures and the whole of nature
in its beauty. The true value of a human being is
determined by the measure and the sense in which they
have obtained liberation from the self.
We shall require a substantially new manner of
thinking if humanity is to survive.
~Albert Einstein*

A Personal Thank You From Jan Gault

If you have finished reading this book, congratulations! You represent a growing number of people who are changing the world for the better. Former Supreme Court Justice Sandra Day O'Connor, in her book *The Majesty of the Law*, wrote, "[C]ourts... are mainly reactive institutions" and "change comes principally from attitudinal shifts in the population at large."

It is genuinely caring people like you who will replace poverty with prosperity, ignorance with enlightened thinking, and violence with compassion. Remember, what we focus on expands. What we visualize and believe—really believe in our hearts—is what we bring into our lives and the world.

Understand: broadening your vision of prosperity for all people in no way precludes your individual hopes and dreams. If you dream of living in a beautiful home, driving a new car, or taking a fabulous vacation, that's wonderful and as it should be. The Bible says, "Ask and you shall receive." Believe and you shall have. Opening your perspective to a better world globally does not mean sacrificing the abundance you desire for yourself and your family. The more you have, the more you can give to others. And the more you give to others, the more you will have. Man and woman were intended to be prosperous and happy.

Truly believe that your choices and actions are making a difference. Keep your vision of global prosperity and an end to poverty and to wars against humanity. Truly believe and act for the happiness and well-being of each person on the face of the earth. And, lo, it will come to pass.

Holding these beliefs in your life will strengthen your heart and mind, and keep you in sync with your "real self," the self of love, compassion, and kindness. I wish you the very best in all your endeavors to create a better life and world. **Dream, Believe, Act, and Receive!**

Warmest Aloha,

Jan

Part IX

Resource Directory

> *What you desire for yourself, we need to desire even more for everyone else in the world.*
> ~Koran

CHOICES FOR A BETTER LIFE, COMMUNITY, AND WORLD

I Choose to . . .

- Embrace this day with enthusiasm, anticipation, and excitement.

- Treat each person I meet with kindness, consideration, and respect.

- Live and laugh, and enjoy any challenges that arise.

- Appreciate and honor the natural beauty that surrounds me.

- Nourish my mind with inspirational and healthy messages.

- Live my values and walk my talk.

- Keep my perspective, and not get sidetracked by pressures and stressors.

- Live fully and richly in the moment—free of past regrets and future concerns.

- Align my actions with my heartfelt desires and dreams.

- Act in the service of those who suffer or who are less fortunate than I am.

- Trust the universe to guide me along the path of purpose and prosperity.

- Perform those activities that empower, enlighten, and energize my life and the lives of others.

Resource Directory

QUOTES TO MOTIVATE AND PROMPT ACTION

*"I am only one,
But still I am one.
I cannot do everything,
But still I can do something.
And because I cannot do everything,
I will not refuse to do the something that I can do."*
~Edward Everett Hale

"The difference between what we do and what we are capable of doing would suffice to solve most of the world's problems."
~Mohandas Gandhi

"Nobody made a greater mistake than he who did nothing because he could do only a little."
~Edmund Burke

"You must do the things you think you cannot do."
~Eleanor Roosevelt

"A life spent making mistakes is not only more honorable but more useful than a life spent in doing nothing."
~George Bernard Shaw

"One act of beneficence, one act of real usefulness, is worth all the abstract sentiment in the world."
~Ann Radcliffe

"Good thoughts are no better than good dreams, unless they be executed."
~Ralph Waldo Emerson

"The world is a dangerous place, not because of those who do evil, but because of those who look on and do nothing."
~Albert Einstein

"A lot of people are waiting for Martin Luther King or Mahatma Gandhi to come back—but they are gone. We are it. It is up to us. It is up to you."
~Marian Wright Edelman

"If you think you're too small to have an impact, try going to bed with a mosquito."
~Anita Roddick

"Magic has often been thought of as the art of making dreams come true, the art of realizing visions. Yet before we can bring birth to the vision, we have to see it."
~Starhawk

"Dreams pass into the reality of action. From the actions stems the dream again; and this interdependence produces the highest form of living."
~Anais Nin

"When everything looks impossible, that's when life offers the greatest opportunities for positive change."
~Juanita Louise Vance

More Actions for a Better Life and World

Actions for Personal-Global Prosperity
Chapter 15 targeted six recommended actions from the list below (identified by *) for Personal-Global Prosperity. Use this list as a reference tool for additional actions you can take.

Help Others to Help Themselves

Action #1:
E-mail and letter-writing campaigns
Subscribe to one of the many organizations that act to persuade Congress to implement programs that get at the root causes of hunger and poverty. For example, instead of giving direct aid to poverty-stricken countries, many organizations help pass legislation that will free money for Third World community development, and provide training in basic job skills, farming, health, and nutrition. Instead of your hard-earned money going to corrupt governments, you are helping people to help themselves. Two organizations which have had impressive results are listed below.

- **Food First Institute for Food and Development Policy**
  This is a nonprofit peoples' think tank and education-for-action center supported by members.
  www.foodfirst.org

- **Bread for the World**
  Bread for the World is comprised of citizens who lobby our nation's decision makers, seeking justice for the world's hungry.
  www.bread.org

Action #2:

Support a micro-lending organization that helps indigenous people to help themselves by giving them small loans to start a business and help their communities. Five of these organizations are listed below:

- **Grameen Bank**
  Grameen Bank was founded by Bangladeshi banker Muhammad Yunus, one of the first lenders to make small loans to the poor. A few dollars can change the fate of a poverty-stricken family in Bangladesh.
  www.grameen-info.org

- **ACCION International**
  Offers credit and training to small entrepreneurs in Latin America and the United States.
  www.accion.org

- **FINCA (Foundation for International Community Assistance)**
  Provides community micro-finance projects in Latin America and Africa.
  www.villagebanking.org

- **Kiva**
  Kiva lets you lend to a specific entrepreneur in a developing country, empowering her to lift herself out of poverty. A loan as small as $25 can make a difference.
  www.kiva.org

- **ModestNeeds.Org**
  This organization seeks to stop poverty before it begins by making small emergency loans to those in need, e.g., to help an individual or family who has had a temporary setback due to an illness or unexpected expense. They also contribute to small worthy nonprofit

organizations. You can support their efforts by making a small donation, by creating a Squidoo lens on the link below (free), by shopping at their CafePress store, as well as with other options.
http://www.modestneeds.org/donation/options
http://www.squidoo.com/modestneeds/hq
http://www.cafepress.com/modestneeds/

Shop for a Better World

Action #3:
Shop for food, clothing, cosmetics, and other products from those corporations which consistently get high marks on social responsibility from consumer rating services. Visit the web sites below for up-to-date information.

- **Business Ethics**
  The site below annually lists one hundred of the most socially responsible corporations. Firms on the list for five recent years (2000-2004) include a diverse array of corporations such as IBM, Intel, Procter & Gamble, Avon Products, Southwest Airlines, Starbucks Coffee, and others.
  www.business-ethics.com

- **Fair Trade Federation (FTF)**
  FTF acts as a clearinghouse for information on fair-trade practices. Its members include wholesalers, retailers, and producers, all of whom provide fair wages and good employment opportunities to economically disadvantaged farmers and artisans around the world.
  www.fairtradefederation.org

- **Multinational Monitor**

  Lists essential information, books, and actions; offers a multinational resource center on-site. An excellent information source for socially responsible companies and other resources.

  www.essential.org/monitor

- **SERRV International**

  SERRV is a nonprofit trade organization that promotes social and economic justice in over forty developing regions throughout the world by providing help in developing and marketing local food products and handcrafts. An online order catalog is available.

  www.serrv.org

- **Council on Economic Priorities**

  In the book *Shopping for a Better World*, the Council lists and rates over 2,500 brand-name products, including packaged food, appliances, computers, toys, clothing, and other consumer goods. Companies are rated according to factors such as their charity records, their environmental responsibility, and whether they promote equal opportunity employment and test products on animals. Check your local library to see if it has a copy of *Shopping for a Better World*.

- **Co-op America—Responsible Shopper**

  This site lets you investigate and compare hundreds of companies on a wide range of issues, including discrimination, sweatshops, ethics, and animal testing. Helps you assess the everyday products you buy, from clothing to cosmetics. Gives ratings for different companies and brands.

  http://tinyurl.com/czxbch

*Action #4:

Purchase food, clothing, books, and other items through a shopping service that will donate a portion of the purchase price to humanitarian organizations.

- Shop for Change

    Buy merchandise through Shop for Change, and a percentage of the purchase price will be donated to progressive organizations such as Educators for Social Responsibility, Alliance for Responsible Trade, National Center for Science Education, Amnesty International, and Physicians for Social Responsibility.

    You can purchase books, organic coffee, music, clothing, and much more from over one hundred online stores at no extra cost to you.

    Each time you purchase merchandise from one of the retailers on this site, Shop for Change will donate up to 5 percent of the purchase price to progressive causes. Retailers include Barnes & Noble, Lands' End, Gaiam.com, Gardener's Supply Company, Uncommon Goods, and others.

    www.credoaction.com

- Practical Action (PA)

    Practical Action is a development charity working with poor people in India, Africa, and Latin America, to help them develop the skills and tools necessary to build a better life. It was founded in 1966 by economist Dr. E. F. Schumacher, based on his philosophy that small changes can make a big difference.

    Help raise money for PA by shopping at Amazon, eBay, or CharityFlowers, or using the Everyclick web site.
    http://practicalaction.org/?id=giveasyoushop

Action #5:

Help indigent peoples in India by shopping at a nonprofit internet store for Indian products such as sarees, dhotis, casual wear, kashmiri, shawls, and much more.

- India Shop is promoted by the Foundation of Occupational Development (FOOD), a twenty-year-old nonprofit organization based in Chennai (South India), which is implementing social development programs to help the poor.
http://www.xlweb.com/indiashop/

Keep Our Environment Healthy

Action #6:

Make a small donation to help end the trend toward global warming that is depleting our water supplies and endangering the survival of life on our planet. Visit the following web site to make your contribution.

- **Nature Conservancy Adopt-An-Acre**
Help protect rain forests and biological diversity by adopting an acre for as little as $50. You'll receive information on the projects you're supporting, along with a *Certificate of Recognition* acknowledging your contribution. Since its inception, the program has protected more than six hundred thousand acres of rain forests in the Caribbean and Latin America. This would make a terrific group project for your school or service organization.
http://tinyurl.com/c7uaxb

*Action #7:

On your next road vacation trip, rent a car from the eco-friendly travel club listed below, which sends 1 percent of its annual revenues to environmental clean-up efforts. You will also receive a discount on hybrid car rentals. Other services include emergency roadside assistance, auto/home insurance, and trip planning.

- **Better World Club**
  www.betterworldclub.com

Action #8:

Help protect our ecosystems while traveling, by making the choice to be a more responsible tourist on your next business or vacation trip. Ecosystems are being threatened by big developments being built to accommodate increased tourism. While traveling, support locally owned hotels and beds-and-breakfasts, whenever possible. Dine at mom and pop restaurants, and patronize other local businesses that are giving back to the community. Remember: what we do in one country affects the ecosystems of other countries—our own included!

Action #9:

Support the Kyoto Agreement: a framework laid down by thirty-eight developed countries to prevent global warming. Let your government officials and local media know where you stand. See the United Nations site below for more information.

- http://unfccc.int/2860.php

Action #10:

Join with like-minded friends to initiate a project on the planting and usage of medicinal plants. Using organic methods, plant gardens of herbs (useful in herbal medicine), fruit, vegetables, and flowers. Help lower-income or homeless women in your community set up and sell some of the products. What is your community doing?

Help Fund Causes You Believe In

Action #11:

Shop at a virtual shopping mall where up to 15 percent of the purchase price will go to a cause of your choice, at no extra cost to you. At the site below, you can shop at over one hundred online stores, including Barnes & Noble, Nordstrom, Dell, OfficeMax, and Lands' End.

- GreaterGood.com
  http://www.greatergood.com

Action #12:

Shop for a cause. Shop at one of the sponsoring merchants on the site below, and a portion of your purchase price will go toward breast cancer research.

- http://preview.tinyurl.com/4n4s

Shop to Raise Money for Your Group, School, or Organization

Action #13:

Do fund-raising for your group, school, or organization by shopping at a virtual mall in which participating business partners contribute a percentage of your purchases.

    The site below offers a diverse range of products, including clothing, toys, electronics, flowers, gifts, and much more.

- http://www.greatergood.com

Action #14:

Fund-raise for your school by shopping at major retail stores. See the site below for full details.

- www.onecause.com

Action #15:

Shop with more than 150 retailers to earn money for your designated religious or cultural organization, charity, or school. The average retailer's contribution to your cause is 7 percent. There is no cost to join for individuals or nonprofit organizations.

- http://www.benevolink.com/

Support Your Local and International Charities by Shopping Online

Action #16:

Support the charity of your choice by shopping. The site below allows you to shop at over four hundred major retailers and specialty shops throughout the United States, and will return a portion of what you spend to your designated cause.

- www.iGive.com

Eat to Save the Earth and Improve Your Health

****Action #17:***

Eat to save the earth and improve your health.
By increasing your diet of organic vegetables and fruits, you not only lower your risk of atherosclerotic heart disease and breast and colon cancer,

but you will also aid prevention of water pollution. Water pollution from such things as pesticides, fertilizer, and manure contaminates more rivers and streams than do all the wastes from United States industries and cities combined.

- **International Vegetarian Union**
  http://www.ivu.org/

Sustain Global Prosperity through Your Financial Institutions

Action #18:
Find out where your bank is investing your money.
Compare your bank's rating with those of other banks. Ratings are based on a diverse range of social and environmental issues and range from Excellent to Poor. Find out how your bank fares, and where your money goes while you sleep. Check the web site below for ratings. If your current bank's rating is not Excellent or Good, consider changing your account to another financial institution. Call your bank and speak with the manager to find out your bank's rating for the last year. For more information, see the web site below.

- **Federal Financial Institutions Examination Council (FFIEC)**
  www.ffiec.gov

Action #19:
Invest in SRIs (Socially Responsible Investments)
Align your financial goals with your personal values by investing in socially responsible money market funds. Typical social screens used are Weapons/Defense, Gambling, Liquor, Tobacco, Nuclear Power, Fair Hiring Policies and Practices, Environmental Responsibility, Products/Services that enhance the quality of life, and International Development.

Resource Directory

How do SRIs perform? Many have outperformed nonSRIs. Overall in the last decade, SRIs have returned an average 9.1 percent a year compared with 9.4 percent average for all U.S. stock funds.[1] Others have performed significantly better. The United Nations has recently officially endorsed SRIs as the international standard. Choose from over one hundred SRIs. Several of these funds with different screens are listed below:

- **Winslow Green** serves high-net-worth individual investors and institutions by investing in environmentally conscious companies. They have been doing "green" investing since 1983.
www.winslowgreen.com

- **Pax World Women's Equity Fund** invests in forward-thinking companies. It also seeks to advance equality, promote peace, and protect the environment.
http://www.paxworld.com/funds/womens-equity-fund

- **Amana Funds** makes investments in companies that adhere to Islamic principles.
www.amanafunds.com

- All of **Pax World's Funds** have a $250 minimum initial investment. Choose from Balanced Funds, Growth Funds, High Yield Funds, and Women's Equity Mutual Funds, among others.
www.paxworld.com

- **The Calvert Group** selects socially and environmentally conscious mutual funds.
http://www.calvertgroup.com/

Need more information or help selecting SRI funds? Check out the two web sites below:

- **Social Funds** is a comprehensive personal finance web site with reports, statistics, performance ratings, and news on a variety of socially responsible investments.
  http://tinyurl.com/cefvrn

- **Natural Investments LLC (NI)**
  NI pioneered socially responsible investing in the 1980s, and works on a management fee basis. Hal and Jack Brill, founders, are the authors of *Investing From the Heart* and *Investing With Your Values*. See their web site for full information.
  www.naturalinvesting.com

Action #20:
Invest in socially responsible stocks.

Perhaps you prefer to invest in individual socially responsible stocks. To view a list of socially responsible and irresponsible corporations, rated according to social and environmental issues such as discrimination in the workplace and global warming, see the web sites below. Make your investments count toward a healthier environment and a more just and humane economy.

- **Ecomall.com** is an excellent site that lists SRI industries and companies.
  http://www.ecomall.com/biz/menu$.htm

- **Domini Social Investments** manages the Domini Social Equity Fund, the first and largest socially and environmentally screened index fund in the world, along with the Domini Social Bond Fund and Domini Money Market Account.
  www.domini.com

Action #21:

Support micro-entrepreneurs in developing countries through your investments.

The same firm listed just above invests in community development. Put some of your investment money into a socially screened mutual fund, which sends a portion of your annual return to support micro-businesses in developing countries.

- Domini Social Investments
  www.domini.com

Action #22:

Buy your personal and business checks from a firm that donates a portion of the printing cost to an organization which you designate.

Order checks from a firm that donates a portion of the money you pay for printing to the organization you designate, such as PETA, Human Rights Campaign, NOW, Sierra Club, National Abortion and Reproductive Rights Action League (NARAL), and many others. Check the web site below for pricing and list of organizations.

- Message Products
  www.messageproducts.com

Action #23:

Switch to a credit card that sends a portion of the money you spend to human rights groups.

Use a credit card that donates a portion of the amount of money you spend to human rights organizations such as Amnesty International, Human Rights Campaign, and Oxfam Canada. One of these is provided on the next page.

- **Citizens Bank Shared Interests VISA**
  Choose from a number of organizations. Every time you use your Amnesty Visa or Oxfam Visa, Citizens Bank will donate ten cents to the organization, along with $20 upon approval of your application.
  www.citizensbank.ca

Action #24:
Switch to a long-distance telephone service that donates some of your money to human rights organizations.

Use a long-distance service that donates a portion of the money you pay for long-distance calls to a human rights organization such as Oxfam Canada and Amnesty International.

- **Working Assets** offers long-distance, credit card, internet, and broadcasting services.
  www.wald.com

Purchase Gifts that Empower People and Protect Our Planet

The gifts you give not only make a statement about your values, but can promote cultural prosperity, helping others to help themselves.

Action #25:
Buy gifts, services, and products from those shops and organizations that are helping others to help themselves.

- **Ten Thousand Villages**
  Purchase unique, fair-trade, handcrafted gifts made by people around the world. Visit their web site to find a store in your area. Your purchase makes a difference!
  www.tenthousandvillages.com

- **Alternative Gifts International**
  Buy gifts that empower people in crisis, protect our planet, and build peace. A few examples of alternative gifts you'll find here:
  - Build a School in Afghanistan
  - Help Endangered Girls in Cambodia
  - Buy a Book—Train a Teacher in Haiti
  - Rescue an Orphan in China
  - Solar Water Pumps in Latin America
  - Eye Service for the Poor in Honduras

- Giving a value gift for a birthday, anniversary, or other occasion, will help build a partnership with those in need, and promote global goodwill. www.altgifts.org

Action #26:
Help struggling families in developing countries help themselves. Give a gift that changes lives.
Donate a cow that provides a needy family with milk, chickens that give fresh eggs, and other livestock to help lift them out of poverty.

- **Heifer Project International Gift Catalog**
  www.heifer.org

Action #27:
Give gifts that support Native American community wellness, eyesight programs in Tibet and Tanzania, and community self-development among indigenous peoples of Guatemala and Chiapas, Mexico. See the site below for a free catalog and complete information.

- **Seva Foundation**
  www.seva.org

Keep Your Home and Family Safe and Healthy

Action #28:

Avoid toxic cleaning products that contain chlorine, ethyl benzene and triclosan (found in detergents and lotions). Protect your health by using vegetable-based cleaning products that work just as well as toxic chemical cleansers. Visit the sites below for natural cleansers and alternatives to chemicals.

- **Gaiam**
  www.gaiam.com

- **Safer Cleaning Products**
  http://www.watoxics.org

- **Alternatives to Chemicals**
  http://tinyurl.com/dlko4k

Action #29:

Check out less toxic pesticide alternatives to protect your home, family, and environment. See the web sites below for options.

- **The Audubon Guide to Home Pesticides**
  http://www.audubon.org/bird/pesticides

- **Environment Canada**
  http://www.ns.ec.gc.ca/

- **Gaiam** has sonic pest-repellers that are eco-safe and reasonably priced. Keep your home free from dangerous chemicals.
  www.gaiam.com

Make Choices that Prevent Animal Abuse

In a world beset with human suffering and problems, it's easy to neglect some of the simple choices that could make a difference in reducing the suffering and pain of dogs, cats, and other animals.

Action #30:

In making your donations to health charities, support those that use alternative methods and avoid funding medical research that involves experimentation on animals. The web sites below list those charities that do and don't fund experimentation on animals.

- http://tinyurl.com/d566j1

See the site below for a report by The Physicians Committee for Responsible Medicine on why medical research does not need to involve animals. A variety of methods are available that are providing better ways to find cures for human diseases.

- HumaneSeal
  http://www.humaneseal.org/research.html

Action #31:

Buy household products, perfumes, cosmetics, and clothing from companies that do not test on animals. Support those firms that aren't abusing and torturing animals. The web site below lists companies who do and don't test on animals.

- http://tinyurl.com/7fs4t

ACTIONS FOR BETTER GLOBAL COMMUNICATION AND UNDERSTANDING

Chapter 16 targeted six recommended actions from the list below (identified by *) for better communication and understanding. Use this list as a reference tool for additional actions you can take.

Take a Reality Tour

Action #1:
Take a reality tour with like-minded people and learn firsthand about a country of interest. What breakthroughs have they had in conflict resolution or putting an end to social and economic injustices? Converse with community leaders and locals. Check the web site below for dates and prices.

- **Global Exchange**
  Meet with community leaders in Ireland, Cuba, Haiti, or South Africa. Talk with locals and participate in community projects.
  www.globalexchange.org/tours

Volunteer for a Global Service Trip

Action #2:
Volunteer some time to work in another country to help foster friendships and build cultural goodwill. A list of web sites is provided below. Select one that aligns with your values and lifestyle.

- **Habitat for Humanity International**
  An ecumenical Christian organization that helps families in the U.S. and other countries build affordable housing. Volunteer for one- to three-week trips.
  www.habitat.org

- **Global Citizens Network**
  Offers one- to three-week service trips around the world. Be part of a group working on projects initiated by locals in the community. Projects range from teaching business skills to setting up a library or health clinic.
  www.globalcitizens.org

- **Global Volunteers**
  Spend one to three weeks working in countries such as Ireland, India, Australia, or Costa Rica. Volunteer your time in local communities to teach, provide health care, do environmental work, construction, childcare, or tutoring. No specialized skills are required.
  www.globalvolunteers.org

- **Cross-Cultural Solutions**
  An international volunteer organization with programs in such countries as China, Russia, Tanzania, India, and Thailand. Participate in community development projects with local people.
  www.crossculturalsolutions.org

- **Action Without Borders**
  Action Without Borders is independent of any government, or political or religious creed. Learn about events and volunteer opportunities in countries throughout the world, such as Chile and New Zealand. Connect with people around the world who share your interests and goals. Its web site includes a Career Center, Resources for Teachers, Tools for Nonprofit Organizations, Tips for Volunteers, and much more!
  www.idealist.org

Participate in a Cultural Exchange Program

Action #3:
Participate in a cultural exchange program to increase your knowledge and understanding of another culture. Check out the two web sites provided below.

- **American Field Service International (AFS)**
  AFS is an international exchange program that focuses on diversity, tolerance, and global citizenship. AFS sends teachers, educators, and students to over fifty countries.
  www.afs.org

- **Council on International Educational Exchange (CIEE)**
  CIEE has voluntary service and work exchange programs for teachers and students.
  www.ciee.org

Join an Online Forum for Intercultural Cooperation and Understanding

Action #4:
Join an online women's forum to exchange information and resources with women in other countries. Make new friendships and share ideas and interests. Explore the women's web sites below to find one compatible with your values and interests.

- **Feminist Majority Foundation (FMF)**
  FMF, founded in 1987, is dedicated to women's equality, reproductive health, and nonviolence. Through research and action, FMF seeks to empower women economically, socially, and politically.
  www.feminist.org

- **MADRE**
  MADRE is an international women's human rights organization, with programs addressing issues that include self-determination and collective rights, community improvement and women's health, discrimination, racism, and human rights education.
  www.madre.org

- **International Federation of University Women (IFUW)**
  An international nongovernmental organization (NGO) of over 150,000 women university graduates, founded in 1919 to promote international friendship, cooperation, and peace.
  www.ifuw.org

Action #5:
Exchange information with like-minded people around the world through an online information forum with an aim toward promoting dialogue and international cooperation. See web site below to get started.

- Mandat International (MI)
  MI is a nonprofit organization, the mission of which is to promote dialogue and international cooperation. Its web site includes a calendar of international meetings and conventions, information on skills exchange and volunteering, plus over one thousand useful links.
  www.mandint.org

Action #6:
Discover positive actions people are taking around the globe. Relate your thoughts and experiences about current events, or ask questions about other people's countries. See the Global Heroes online forum.

- **Global Heroes**
  Highlights the positive in the world and profiles global heroes and what they're doing in their countries. Has an online forum on which you can post announcements, relate experiences, or ask questions relating to different countries or current events.
  www.globalheroes.com

Take a Vacation that Promotes Intercultural Understanding

Billions of dollars are spent each year on vacation travel. What impact are your vacation activities having on people in the countries you visit?

Vacations are an excellent time to share information and learn more about another culture. How you spend your time and money on a vacation reflects your values.

Action #7:
Set aside some of your vacation time to visit or stay with locals. Register with one of the international host networks and arrange to share a meal or stay at a local home. Experience other cultures more deeply than just as "a tourist." One of these is given below:

- **SERVAS International**
  Visit foreign countries and communicate with people in different cultures on real issues. SERVAS was founded in 1949 and has members in over 130 countries who will welcome you into their homes. Person-to-person contacts can make an important difference in building world peace and understanding. A small annual fee is charged to register with SERVAS.
  www.servas.org

Action #8:

On your next vacation, rather than staying in hotels, exchange your home with that of someone from another country. You'll have many countries and times to choose from at the site listed below.

- **Home Exchange**
  www.homeexchange.com

Action #9:

Take a cultural tour on your vacation to enhance your understanding of the world and its people. Short tours and affordable trips are offered by the travel agent listed below.

- **Travel Concepts International: Cultural Tours to Better Understand the World and Its People**
  Now offering "Between Weekends"—shorter, moderately priced tours for couples, families, and solo travelers.
  www.tci-travel.com

Action #10:

While on vacation, check out local community organizations and arrange to attend one of their meetings. You can find these listed in local newspapers, or check local online web sites. Select one that shares your values and interests.

Give Gifts that Teach Children Respect and Cooperation

Action #11:
Enrich the lives of children by giving gifts that teach cooperation and respect, and inspire creativity. Choose from a vast array of products for boys and girls of all ages. See web site below.

- Hearth Song
  www.hearthsong.com

Celebrate Diversity

*Action #12:
How much cultural diversity is reflected in your home? Check out the literature, music, crafts, and artwork in your home. Assess what kind of statement you're making when others visit you. Do you want to eliminate anything or add something new?

Action #13:
Shop at an ethnic market or grocery store in your community. Take time to chat with the owners and learn about their families.

Action #14:
Attend a dance performance or stage play, or listen to music by artists whose ethnicity and background is different from your own. Express appreciation for the ways in which it touched you or expanded your perspective.

Action #15:
Learn how to cook a traditional dinner from another culture. Invite family and friends to share with you.

Resource Directory

Speak Out for Your Values

Action #16:

When you hear ethnic, gender, or racial slurs, speak up. Without being judgmental, let others know where you stand. Speak kindly and gently, but with firmness. Compassion is catching.

Action #17:

Respond to media articles that present cultural misinformation, partial information, or biased views. Let the public know the other side. If not you, who?

Action #18:

Use the medium of public television to express your views. Record a short audio- or videotape and have it aired on public TV. It's easy and economical (free).

Build Peace and Cooperation in Children through the Gifts You Give

*Action #19:

Buy toys, games, books, and music for your children, grandchildren, nieces, and nephews that celebrate cultural diversity and nonviolence. Refuse to buy guns, and games that promote hatred and revenge.

Welcome Differences

Action #20:

Check out the web site below to learn about more ways you can become an ambassador of goodwill and understanding.

- Southern Poverty Law Center
  www.tolerance.org

Fun and Friendship

Action #21:
If you are a woman over fifty, click on the web site below to join one of the fastest-growing groups in the world. Their only mission is to promote fun and friendship. Cost to join is nil to nominal. Make contacts with women in countries around the world. Friendship has power, and we need to keep some fun in our lives to revitalize us.

- **Red Hat Society**
  www.redhatsociety.com

Actions for a Sounder and Saner Education

Chapter 17 targeted six recommended actions from the list below (identified by *) for Education. Please use this list as a reference tool for additional actions you can take.

Stay Informed about Vital Global Issues

Action #1:
Keep yourself and your family informed about global issues with quality books and media. Visit your library, or rent or order books listed in the Resource Directory's Bibliography at the end of this book. You might also want to check out one of the socially responsible publishers listed below, to place an order.

- **Heartsong Books**
  Heartsong is a publisher of books that celebrate the interconnectedness of life. It offers books of inspiration, compassion, and spirit. Its web site also lists multicultural children's books.
  www.heartsongbooks.com

- **New Society Publishers**
  New Society publishes books for fundamental social change through nonviolent action.
  www.newsociety.com

- **Nation Books**
  Nation Books is a progressive publisher with books on the social and cultural forces shaping our lives. Books are available on human rights, art and culture, feminism, race, environment, and much more.
  http://www.nationbooks.org/

Keep Abreast of Human Rights Projects and Get Involved

Action #2:
Register online with one of the hundreds of human rights organizations listed in a global web directory, in order to receive up-to-date information on activities and issues around the world.

- DMOZ (Directory Mozilla)
  A massive public web directory of human rights organizations that is compiled and edited by a vast global community of volunteer editors.
  http://preview.tinyurl.comcbv6ge

Action #3:
Attend a training center for human rights and peace teaching. Conferences are held annually, especially for teachers, educators, and NGO representatives. Check out the web site below.

- International Training Centre for Human Rights and Peace Teaching (CIFEDHOP)/World Association for the School as an Instrument of Peace (EIP)
  http://preview.tinyurl.com/dfwv5q

Action #4:
Visit a web resource center that has online forums and databases on human rights education. See below.

- Electronic Resource Centre for Human Rights Education Associates (HREA)
  This is an online repository of human rights education and training materials. HREA has online forums, databases, and links to other organizations and resources. Materials are free of charge. Forums

include Global Human Rights Education (listserv) through which educators and advocates exchange information on studies, training, and conferences. There are approximately three thousand organizations and individuals from over 150 countries in this forum. www.hrea.org/erc

***Action #5:**
Subscribe to Amnesty International's Human Rights Education Newsletter and take action in minutes on educational issues of concern. Let your voice be heard!

- www.amnesty.org

Action #6:
Network with human rights education professionals to promote human rights ideals.

- **Human Rights Education Associates (HREA)**
  HREA is an international NGO that works with individuals and organizations to implement human rights education programs. Programs seek to promote attitudes and actions that will protect human rights, and foster free and just communities.
  http://www.hrea.org/

Expand Your Mind by Exploring Alternative Media

Action #7:
Expand your mind by exploring media with different viewpoints. Read and tune in to alternative media that give more in-depth coverage of global issues affecting us all.

- **Papipaul Organization**
  A listing of media links that provides alternatives to mainstream media.
  http://www.papipaul.org/

- **New Dimensions World Broadcasting Network (ND)**
  Founded in 1973, ND is a nonprofit, public benefit, educational corporation, with worldwide radio broadcasts heard by more than one million people. ND seeks a more just and compassionate world through deep dialogues with individuals actively engaged in making a creative contribution to the world. Interviews have included the late Joseph Campbell, physicist David Bohn, Pulitzer prize winners E.O. Wilson from Harvard and poet/ecologist Gary Snyder. ND publishes a newsletter, audiotapes, and a number of books based on the dialogues.
  www.newdimensions.org

- **The Nation**
  A nonpartisan weekly magazine for progressives. Critically discusses political and social questions in an attempt to avoid the misrepresentation and exaggeration found in much political writing of today.
  www.thenation.com

- **Utne Reader**
  Utne reprints provocative writing from diverse perspectives with articles from over two thousand alternative media sources on the latest ideas and trends emerging in our culture. Sign up to receive free newsletters on science, politics, media, and more.
  www.utne.com

- **Guardian Unlimited**

    A progressive newspaper based in the United Kingdom. An excellent online resource for world news and events.

    www.guardian.co.uk/

- **TomPaine.com**

    TomPaine.com is based in Washington, D.C., and was founded in 1995 by John Moyers to take on controversial issues often not covered by mainstream media. Highlights news and ideas to keep you informed.

    www.tompaine.com

- **Positive Futures Network**

    Positive Futures Network publishes *Yes! A Journal of Positive Futures*. Supports those people dedicated to creating a just, sustainable, and compassionate future.

    www.futurenet.org

Learn Innovative Methods by Attending a Conference on Social Change

Action #8:

Attend a conference on social change. It will broaden your horizons, and open your mind to new possibilities and innovative ideas for change. Check the institute below for conference dates.

- **Institute of Cultural Affairs Worldwide**

    A nonprofit organization concerned with the human factor in world development. Lists annual conferences and a volunteer program.

    http://www.ica-international.org/

Take a Class in Ecology with Like-Minded Adults

Action #9:

Interested in ecological studies? Take a two- or three-week course on a subject of interest with like-minded adult students from around the world. For a list of courses, current schedule, fees, and other information, see the web site below.

- **Schumacher College**
  Schumacher College, founded in 1991, is an international centre for ecological studies located in the beautiful Devonshire countryside of England. Students, aged 20 to 80, come from all over the world to attend forward thinking classes such as "Transformative Learning," "Holistic Perspectives on Health," "Culture and Empowerment," "Global Business Ethics," and "Holistic Science." Schumacher College believes "that a new vision is needed for society, its values and its relationship to the earth."
  http://www.schumachercollege.org.uk

Promote Health Education and Empowerment in Underdeveloped Countries

***Action #10:**

Aid health education and empowerment in underdeveloped countries. If you are interested in health education in underdeveloped countries, you'll want to visit the Hesperian Foundation site listed below. It offers a number of ongoing volunteer projects. Read the current newsletter online, and learn about the many activities in which you can become involved.

- **Hesperian Foundation**
  The Hesperian Foundation is a nonprofit publisher of books and

newsletters for community-based health care and empowerment. They publish *Where Women Have No Doctor* and *Where There Is No Doctor*, books that have been widely used in underdeveloped, poverty-stricken countries in which the vast majority of the people do not have access to medical facilities.

www.hesperian.org

Help End Illiteracy in Underdeveloped Countries

*Action #11:
Make a donation of air miles to help end illiteracy in Central America. A donation of fifty thousand points through American, Continental, Delta, Taca, or United Air Lines for the round-trip will support book deliveries in Central and South American communities. Check out the web site below for detailed information on this and other ways to support the education of elementary children in Central and South America.

- **Books for a Better World (BBW)**
  BBW is an organization designed to end illiteracy in developing countries—a major factor in the dependence of developing countries on foreign financial assistance. Books for a Better World seeks to motivate and empower children in developing countries through establishing libraries and scholarship programs.
  http://www.booksforabetterworld.org

Join a Discussion Forum on an Educational Issue of Interest

Action #12:
Share ideas with others on a specific topic of interest.
Visit the site on the next page, and click on one of the many dedicated

organizations to learn more about a topic of interest and what you can do to make a difference.

- **Grassroots.org**

    Grassroots.org is a 501(c)(3) charitable corporation run by unpaid volunteers. The site offers discussion forums, resources, and an extensive list of excellent links to humanitarian organizations dealing with education, the homeless, consumer protection, environmentalism, humanitarian relief, and much more. There are no sales and promotion of products at this web site. You will find clear, objective information used by global citizens throughout the world.
    www.grassroots.org

Become Involved in "Conflict Evolution"

*Action #13:
Visit the site below and discover how "Conflict Evolution" in theatre and other arts is being successfully used to teach children and youth about peace—within themselves and with others. This is a program based in Ontario, Canada, and its successful techniques are greatly in demand. If you are interested in peace building, this is a site you'll definitely want to check out.

- www.childrenspeacetheatre.org

Promote Multicultural Awareness
Via Classroom Global Collaboration

*Action #14:
Promote multicultural awareness through international learning teams. The site below is dedicated to promoting multicultural awareness

by connecting K-12 classrooms worldwide into international learning teams. Click to discover how you can participate in this project to make the world a better place. Friends and Flags is headquartered in Israel.

- **Global SchoolNet
  Friends and Flags**
  http://www.gsn.org/programs/friendsandflags or www.friendsandflags.org

Learn More about How We Can Better Educate Our Children for the 21st Century

Action #15:
Read Riane Eisler's book, *Tomorrow's Children: A Blueprint for Partnership Education for the 21st Century.* Check your library or click on the web site below for reviews and order information.

- http://tinyurl.com/ctr2wx

Educate Yourself on a Specific Global Topic of Interest

Action #16:
Reduce global suffering by educating yourself on a specific global issue of interest, in order to position yourself for helping others. Check out your topic of interest on the internet, at the library, or via social media sources.

> *Education is the Most Powerful Weapon
> Which You Can Use To Change the World.*
> ~Nelson Mandela

Resource Directory

THREE ACTIONS YOU ARE TAKING FOR PERSONAL-GLOBAL EMPOWERMENT AND PROSPERITY

1._____
_____
_____
_____

Date Taken_____

2._____
_____
_____
_____

Date Taken_____

3._____
_____
_____
_____

Date Taken_____

Signed by_____
Please Print Name Clearly _____
Your Email Address (optional) _____

Please Email to prosper@drjan.net

GLOBAL CITIZEN PLEDGE*

I am part of a "vital unity linking me with all humanity and humanity with all life, and I resolve to act accordingly so that each may prosper and all may continue."
~Bill Sander

As a Global Person, I pledge to . . .

- Be proactive and stay informed about the ways in which my daily activities can make a difference in lives around the world.
- Begin with myself; knowing that only by taking care of my own mental, emotional, spiritual, and physical health can I be an effective agent of change. Only then can I set a good example for others.
- Serve my community in ways that benefit all.
- Keep an open mind to ideological differences and practices, searching for common ground and possibilities for cooperation.
- Appreciate and learn from differences. I will strive to be nonjudgmental and accepting, looking for the best in others, and resolving through nonviolent means any conflicts that arise.
- Hold a sustainable vision of world prosperity, universal education, socioeconomic justice, and peace.

_____   _____
           Signed by   Date

Your Email Address (optional) _____

Please Email to prosper@drjan.net or sign online at:
http://www.drjan.net/globalpledge

Reprinted from Quotes, Questions & Actions for Global Understanding by Jan Gault, 2006

Bibliography:
Books Making a Global Difference

Bibliography:
Books Making a Global Difference

Anderson, Walter Truett. *The Next Enlightenment: Integrating East and West in a New Vision of Human Evolution.* St. Martin's Press, 2003.

Barlow, Maude. *Global Showdown: How the New Activists Are Fighting Global Corporate Rule.* Stoddart Publishing, 2002. (out of print)

Bornstein, David. *How to Change the World: Social Entrepreneurs and the Power of New Ideas.* Oxford University Press, 2007.

Brill, Hal, Jack A. Brill, and Cliff Feigenbaum. *Investing With Your Values.* New Society Publishers, 2000.

Brokaw, Tom. "Foreword." In *Be the Change! Change the World, Change Yourself*, edited by Michelle Nunn. Hundreds of Heads Books, 2006.

Canfield, Jack, Mark Victor Hansen, Candice C. Carter, Susanna Palomares, Linda K. Williams, and Bradley L. Winch. *Chicken Soup for the Soul Stories for a Better World.* Health Communications, Inc, 2005.

Coelho, Paulo. *The Alchemist: A Fable About Following Your Dream.* Bt Bound, 2001.

Daley-Harris, Shannon, Jeffrey Keenan, and Karen Speerstra. *Our Day to End Poverty: 24 Ways You Can Make a Difference.* Berrett-Koehler Publishers, 2007.

Derickson, Rossella, and Krista Henley. *Awakening Social Responsibility: A Call to Action Guidebook for Global Citizens, Corporate and Nonprofit Organizations.* Happy About, 2007.

Edgerton, Robert B. *Sick Societies: Challenging the Myth of Primitive Harmony.* Free Press, 1992.

Eisler, Riane. *The Power of Partnership: Seven Relationships That Will Change Your Life*. New World Library, 2002.

Eisler, Riane. *The Chalice and the Blade: Our History, Our Future*. Harper, 1988.

Fisher-McGarry, Julie. *Be the Change You Want to See in the World: 365 Things You Can Do for Yourself and Your Planet*. Conari Press, 2006.

Florida, Richard. *The Rise of the Creative Class*. Basic Books, 2002.

Fresco, Jacque. *The Best That Money Can't Buy: Beyond Politics, Poverty, & War*. Global Cybervisions, 2002.

Fuller, Robert W. *Somebodies and Nobodies: Overcoming the Abuse of Rank*. New Society Publishers, 2003.

Gandhi, Arun, ed. *World without Violence: World Leaders Share Their Commentaries on World Harmony, Peace and Justice*. M.K. Gandhi Institute for Nonviolence, 1999.

Gault, Jan L. *Free Time: Making Your Leisure Count*. Wiley & Sons, 1983.

Gault, Jan L. *The Mighty Power of Your Beliefs*. Ocean Manor, 2000.

Gault, Jan L. *Motivational Messages for Miracle Moments*. Ocean Manor, 2007.

Gault, Jan L. *Quotes, Questions & Actions for Global Understanding*. Ocean Manor, 2006.

Gearon, Liam. *Human Rights Handbook: A Global Perspective for Education*. Trentham Books Ltd., 2003.

Gladwell, Malcolm. *The Tipping Point: How Little Things Can Make a Big Difference*. Back Bay Books, 2002.

Harman, Willis. *Global Mind Change: The Promise of the 21st Century*. Berrett-Koehler Publishing, 1998.

Harrison, Lawrence E., and Samuel P. Huntington, eds. *Culture Matters: How Values Shape Human Progress*. Basic Books, 2000.

Henderson, Hazel. *Creating Alternative Futures*. Kumarian Press, 1996.

Henderson, Hazel, and Simran Sethi. *Ethical Markets: Growing the Green Economy*. Chelsea Green Publishing, 2007.

Henderson, Hazel, and Daisaku Ikeda. *Toward an Age of Light: Building a Brighter Future for Our Global Family*. Middleway Press, 2004.

Holland, Gail Bernice. *A Call For Connection: Solutions for Creating a Whole New Culture*. New World Library, 1998.

Hubbard, Barbara Marx. *Conscious Evolution: Awakening the Power of Our Social Potential*. New World Library, 1998.

Hubbard, Barbara Marx. *Emergence: The Shift from Ego to Essence: 10 Steps to the Universal Human*. Walsch Books, 2001.

Inglehart, Ronald, and Pippa Norris. *Rising Tide: Gender Equality and Cultural Change Around the World*. Cambridge University Press, 2003.

Jones, Ellis, Ross Haenfler, Brett Johnson, and Brian Klocke. *The Better World Handbook—From Good Intentions to Everyday Actions*. New Society Publishers, 2001.

Kumar, Satish. *You Are, Therefore I Am: A Declaration of Dependence*. Green Books, 2002.

Laszlo, Ervin. *You Can Change the World: The Global Citizen's Handbook for Living on Planet Earth*. Select Books, 2003.

Lipton, Bruce H. *Biology of Belief.* Mountain of Love/Elite Books, 2005.

Mayo, Marjorie. *Global Citizens: Social Movements and the Challenge of Globalization.* Illus. ed. Zed Books, 2005.

Mayor, Federico, and Jerome Binde. *The World Ahead: Our Future in the Making.* Zed Books, 2001.

Milord, Susan. *Hands Around the World: 365 Creative Ways to Encourage Cultural Awareness and Global Respect.* Williamson Kids Can! Series. Williamson Publishing, 2003.

Nagler, Michael N. *Is There No Other Way? The Search for a Nonviolent Future.* Berkeley Hills Books, 2001.

Norton, Michael. *365 Ways to Change the World: How to Make a Difference One Day at a Time.* Free Press, 2007.

Ogilvy, James A. *Creating Better Futures: Scenario Planning As a Tool for Social Creativity.* Oxford Press, 2002.

Ogilvy, James A. *Creating Better Futures: Scenario Planning as a Tool for a Better Tomorrow.* Clarendon Press, 2005.

Petchesky, Rosalind P. *Global Prescriptions: Gendering Health and Human Rights.* Zed Books, 2003.

Priesnitz, Wendy. *Challenging Assumptions in Education.* Alternate Press, 2000.

Quinn, Robert E. *Change the World: How Ordinary People Can Accomplish Extraordinary Results.* Jossey-Bass, Inc., Publishers, 2000.

Rheingold, Howard. *Smart Mobs: The Next Social Revolution.* Perseus Publishing, 2002.

Ritzer, George. *The Globalization of Nothing*. Pine Forge Press, 2003.

Robertson, Geoffrey. *Crimes Against Humanity: The Struggle for Global Justice*. New Press, 2003.

Schlitz, Marilyn Mandala, Cassandra Vieten, and Tina Amorok. *Living Deeply: The Art and Science of Transformation in Everyday Life*. Institute of Noetic Sciences/New Harbinger, 2008.

Schultz, William F. *Tainted Legacy: 9/11 and the Ruin of Human Rights*. Nation Books, 2003.

Schutze, Steffi. *We're Global Citizens: Conversations with Tomorrow's Leaders*. Paraview Special Editions, 2003.

Shostak, Arthur B., ed. *Viable Utopian Ideas: Shaping a Better World*. M. E. Sharpe, 2003.

Seigel, Bernie. *Love, Magic and Mudpies: Raising Your Kids to Feel Loved, Be Kind, and Make a Difference*. Rodale, 2006.

Smith, Stephen C. *Ending Global Poverty: A Guide to What Works*. Palgrave Macmillan, 2005.

Steffen, Alex. *Worldchanging: A User's Guide for the 21st Century*, with foreword by Al Gore. Abrams, 2008

Strong, Maurice. *Where On Earth Are We Going?* Texere, 2001.

Thoele, Sue Patton. *Growing Hope: Sowing the Seeds of Positive Change in Your Life and the World*. Red Wheel/Weiser, 2004.

Toms, Michael. *At the Leading Edge: New Visions of Science, Spirituality, and Society*. Larson Publications, 1991.

Tye, Kenneth. *Global Education: From Thought to Action.* Association for Supervision and Curriculum Development, 1991.

Wallensteen, Peter. *Understanding Conflict Resolution: War, Peace and the Global System.* Sage Publications, 2002.

Walljasper, Jan, Jon Spayde, and the editors of the *Utne Reader. Visionaries:People and Ideas to Change Your Life*, with foreword by Eric Utne. New Society Publishers, 2001.

Williams, Jessica. *50 Facts That Should Change The World.* The Disinformation Company, 2007.

Wolman, Richard N. *Thinking with Your Soul.* Harmony Books, 2001.

World Bank. *The Global Citizen's Handbook: Facing our World's Crises and Challenges.* 1st U.S. ed. Collins, 2007.

Yunus, Muhammad. *Banker to the Poor: Micro-Lending and the Battle Against World Poverty.* Public Affairs, October 2003.

APPENDIX

List of Activities

STEP 1
- *Draft Your Master Vision Statement*

STEP 2
- *Target Areas for Improvement*

STEP 3
Map Out Your Personal-Global Dreams
- Personal-Global Prosperity
- Improving Communication and Understanding
- Creating a Sounder and Saner Education

STEP 4
Challenges to Change . . .
Break Free from Belief Barriers Foiling Your Dreams
- Shed Beliefs Preventing You from Taking Effective Action toward Personal-Global Empowerment and Prosperity
- Break Out of Belief Barriers Permanently—Take Charge of Your Beliefs and Life Now!

STEP 5 / Resource Directory
Actions for Personal-Global Prosperity:
- Help others to help themselves (Actions 1, 2)
- Shop for a better world (Actions 3, 4, 5)
- Keep our environment healthy (Actions 6, 7, 8, 9, 10)
- Help fund causes you believe in (Actions 11, 12)
- Shop to raise money for your group, school, or organization (Actions 13, 14, 15)
- Support your local and international charities by shopping online (Action 16)
- Eat to save the earth and improve your health (Action 17)
- Sustain global prosperity through your financial institutions (Actions 18, 19, 20, 21, 22, 23, 24)
- Purchase gifts that empower people and protect our planet (Actions 25, 26, 27)
- Keep your home and family safe and healthy (Actions 28, 29)
- Make choices that prevent animal abuse (Actions 30, 31)

Actions for Better Global Communication and Understanding
- Take a reality tour (Action 1)
- Volunteer for a global service trip (Action 2)
- Participate in a cultural exchange program (Action 3)
- Join an online forum for intercultural cooperation and understanding (Actions 4, 5, 6)
- Take a vacation that promotes intercultural understanding (Actions 7, 8, 9, 10)
- Give gifts that teach children respect and cooperation (Action 11)
- Celebrate diversity (Actions 12, 13, 14, 15)
- Speak out for your values (Actions 16, 17, 18)

- Build peace and cooperation in children through the gifts you give (Action 19)
- Welcome differences (Action 20)
- Fun and friendship (Action 21)

Actions for a Sounder and Saner Education
- Stay informed about vital global issues (Action 1)
- Keep abreast of human rights projects and get involved (Actions 2, 3, 4, 5, 6)
- Expand your mind by exploring alternative media (Action 7)
- Learn innovative methods by attending a conference on social change (Actions 8)
- Take a class in ecology with like-minded adults (Action 9)
- Promote health education and empowerment in underdeveloped countries (Action 10)
- Help end illiteracy in underdeveloped countries (Action 11)
- Join a discussion forum on an educational issue of interest (Action 12)
- Become involved in "Conflict Evolution" (Action 13)
- Promote multicultural awareness via classroom global collaboration (Action 14)
- Learn more about how we can better educate our children for the twenty-first century (Action 15)
- Educate yourself on a specific global topic of interest (Action 16)

Notes

Global Challenges

1. Women for Women International/Soroptimist International, *Project Independence/Women Survivors of War*, http://becuzwecan.wordpress.com/2008/06/18/project-independence/ (accessed 9 March 2009).

2. Lawrence E. Harrison and Samuel P. Huntington, eds., *Culture Matters: How Values Shape Human Progress* (Basic Books, 2000), xviii.

3. *The World's Women 2000: Trends and Statistics* (United Nations Publications), http://unstats.un.org/unsd/demographic/products/indwm/wwpub2000educ.htm.

4. Ibid.

5. Simmons College School of Social Work, http://web.simmons.edu/~sealey/ghana.pdf, 9 (accessed 9 March 2009).

6. Harrison and Huntington, *Culture Matters*, xix.

7. World Bank, *World Development Indicators 2007*, http://siteresources.worldbank.org/DATASTATISTICS/Resources/WDI07section1-intro.pdf, 4 (accessed 24 April 2007).

8. Environment News Service, http://www.ens-newswire.com/ens/mar2008/2008-03-29-094.asp (accessed 9 March 2009).

9. Water and Waste Water International, World Development Movement, http://www.water-int.com/categories/global-water-crisis/women-and-water-a-truly-global-struggle.asp (accessed 9 March 2009).

10. San Francisco AIDS Foundation, *Women & HIV*, 2006, http://www.sfaf.org/aidsinfo/statistics/global (accessed 13 February 2009).

11. Care, *Women's Day Facts*, http://www.care.org/newsroom/specialreports/women/womens_facts.asp (accessed 19 February 2009).

12. Harrison and Huntington, *Culture Matters*, xviii.

13. Geraldine Bedell, *Make Poverty History: How You Can Help Defeat World Poverty in Seven Easy Steps* (Penguin Books, 2005), 45; http://www.makepovertyhistory.org/docs/book.swf (accessed 9 March 2009).

14. United States Statistics Division, *Statistics and Indicators on Women and Men*, http://unstats.un.org/unsd/demographic/products/indwm/wwpub2000press.htm (accessed 10 March 2009).

15. Council on Foreign Relations, *Summary: A Symposium on Human Trafficking*, http://www.cfr.org/content/meetings/human_trafficking_summary.pdf (accessed 24 April 2007).

16. United States Statistics Division, *Statistics and Indicators on Women and Men*, http://unstats.un.org/unsd/demographic/products/indwm/wwpub2000press.htm (accessed 10 March 2009).

17. Ibid.

18. Sylvanna Falcón, "Rape as a Weapon of War: Advancing Human Rights for Women at the U.S.-Mexico Border," *Social Justice*, Summer 2001, 28:2; Criminal Justice Periodicals; http://www.nlgmltf.org/pdfs/12-falcon-rape-war-mexicop-border.pdf (accessed 10 March 2009).

19. Religious Tolerance Organization, *Rape of Women During Wartime*, http://www.religioustolerance.org/war_rape.htm (accessed 10 March 2009).

20. United States Statistics Division, *Statistics and Indicators on Women and Men*, http://unstats.un.org/unsd/demographic/products/indwm/wwpub2000press.htm (accessed 10 March 2009).

21. Amnesty International, http://www.amnesty.org/en/death-penalty/numbers, http://www.amnesty.org/en/death-penalty/myths-facts/myths, http://www.amnesty.org/en/death-penalty/myths-facts/facts (accessed 10 March 2009).

22. United States Statistics Division, *Statistics and Indicators on Women and Men*, http://unstats.un.org/unsd/demographic/products/indwm/wwpub2000press.htm (accessed 10 March 2009).

23. Anup Shah, "Nature and Animal Conservation," *Global Issues: Social, Political, Economic and Environmental Issues That Affect Us All*, http://www.globalissues.org/article/177/nature-and-animal-conservation (accessed 9 March 2009).

24. Anup Shah, "Climate Change and Global Warming," *Global Issues: Social, Political, Economic and Environmental Issues That Affect Us All*, http://www.globalissues.org/issue/178/climate-change-and-global-warming (accessed 9 March 2009).

Chapter 2

1. Riane Eisler. citing her previous book in *The Power of Partnership: Seven Relationships that Will Change Your Life* (New World Library, 2003), xii.

Chapter 8

1. Ignacio Ramonet, "The Politics of Hunger," *Le Monde diplomatique* (November 1998), http://mondediplo.com/1998/11/01leader (accessed 10 March 2009).

2. Bridget McManamon, "Eliminating Hunger in a World of Plenty," *Bio-Medicine* (5 August 2003), http://news.bio-medicine.org/medicine-news-2/Eliminating-hunger-in-a-world-of-plenty-5975-2/ (accessed 10 March 2009).

3. Robert W. Goodwin, "The Only Journey There Is: An Exploration of Cosmic and Cultural Evolution," *What Is Enlightenment?* (magazine now entitled *EnlightenNext*) (January-March 2007); 70, http://www.enlightennext.org/magazine/.

4. Amnesty International, http://www.amnesty.org/en/death-penalty/numbers (accessed 10 March 2009).

5. Emily Hannum and Claudia Buchmann, *The Consequences of Global Educational Expansion: Social Science Perspectives* (American

Academy of Arts and Sciences, 2003), iii; http://www.amacad.org/publications/monographs/Ubase.pdf (accessed 10 March 2009).

6. Muhammad Yunus, "Banker to the Poor: Micro-Lending and the Battle Against World Poverty," *Public Affairs*, October 2003, 235.

Chapter 10

1. Emily Hannum and Claudia Buchmann, *The Consequences of Global Educational Expansion: Social Science Perspectives* (American Academy of Arts and Sciences, 2003), iv; http://www.amacad.org/publications/monographs/Ubase.pdf (accessed 10 March 2009).

2. Global Campaign for Education, "Learning to Survive: How Education for All Would Save Millions of Young People from HIV/AIDS" (22 April 2004), http://siteresources.worldbank.org/CSO/Resources/Learning_to_Survive_by_Oxfam.pdf, 2 (accessed 10 March 2009).

3. Ibid., 5.

4. United States Statistics Division, *Statistics and Indicators on Women and Men*, http://unstats.un.org/unsd/demographic/products/indwm/wwpub2000press.htm (accessed 10 March 2009).

5. Ignacio Ramonet, "The Politics of Hunger," *Le Monde diplomatique* (November 1998), http://mondediplo.com/1998/11/01leader (accessed 10 March 2009).

Chapter 11

1. Hazel Henderson and Daisaku Ikeda, *Planetary Citizenship* (Middleway Press, 2004), 83.
2. Domestic Violence Resource Center of South County, http://www.wrcsc.org/stats.htm (accessed 10 March 2009).
3. Amnesty International, "Make Some Noise: Campaign Issues Fact Sheet" (AI Media Briefing), 6 December 2005, http://www.amnesty.org/en/library/info/ACT30/025/2005/en or http://tinyurl.com/ca883y.
4. Bruce H. Lipton, *The Biology of Belief* (Mountain of Love/Elite Books, 2005), 13.

Chapter 15

1. Jonathan Clements, "Helping Your Portfolio, Not the World: The Case for Socially Responsible Investments," *Wall Street Journal*, Aug 3, 2005, http://online.wsj.com/article/0,,SB112302218159603090,00.html or http://tinyurl.com/boyaxs.

Chapter 17

1. Lisa Smith and Lawrence Haddad, "Women's Status, Women's Education and Child Nutrition in Developing Countries," International Food Policy Research Institute (July 20, 1999).
2. Randy Hitz, "Early Education Needs Support," *HonoluluAdvertiser.com* (August 21, 2005), http://the.honoluluadvertiser.com/article/2005/Aug/21/op/FP508210307.html.

Appendix

Resource Directory

1. Jonathan Clements, "Helping Your Portfolio, Not the World: The Case for Socially Responsible Investments," *Wall Street Journal*, Aug 3, 2005,
http://online.wsj.com/article/SB112302218159603090.html

Index

A

abundance. *See also* prosperity; scarcity
   aligning beliefs with your soul, 149
   belief and the probability of, 152
   beliefs of prosperity, 76
   co-creator of, 154
   global change and, 72
   global view and personal, 167
   human family and, 68
   personal belief system, 74
   prosperity and, 88
   qualities of, 68
   of resources, 69
Abundant World Harvest Day, 147
ACCION International, 176
Action Without Borders, 130
AFS. *See* American Field Service International (AFS)
Ahmed, Dr. Saleem, v
Alliance for Responsible Trade, 121, 179
Alternative Gifts International, 125, 189
Alternatives to Chemicals, 190
Amana Funds, 123, 185
Amazon, 179

American Field Service International (AFS), 194
Amnesty International, 121, 146, 179, 187
Amnesty International's Human Rights Education Newsletter, 135, 203
animal abuse, 191, 224
The Audubon Guide to Home Pesticides, 190
Aurelius, Marcus, 11

B

Barker, Joel A., 43
Barnes & Noble, 121, 179, 182
BBW. *See* Books for a Better World (BBW)
belief bank
   beliefs, building your, 93–94
   beliefs and life, changing your, 99
   believe in others, 94–95
   believe in yourself, 94–95
   care and compassion, world needs, 97–98
   change by peaceful means, 100–101
   choices do make a difference, 95–96
   ego power vs. inner power, 101

prosperity, everyone deserves, 96–97
social being, you are a, 98
belief barriers. *See also* empowering beliefs
   ability to create positive change or influence, 57–58
   blaming others, 78–79
   discouragement, self-doubts, and frustration, 55
   educational ideals and, 83–84
   everybody gets what they deserve, 73–74
   experts or authorities should do it, 86–87
   family and community first, 79–80
   feeling overwhelmed, 60–61
   foreign aid is the answer, 68
   good guys vs. bad guys, 87–88
   judging others vs. kindness, 79
   judging Third World countries, 80–81
   judgment and communication, 77–78
   lack of confidence in self and abilities, 66
   life is mostly chance and fate, 66
   mental-emotional health, 158
   mind-heart distinctions, 163–67
   the past equals the future, 70
   people are by nature bad, 84–85
   personal responsibility, abdication of, 56–57
   poverty and limited resources, 68
   poverty is due to incompetence, 74–75
   scarcity, 67–68
   self-worth vs. material wealth, 67
   shedding, 62
   superiority of Western culture, 81–82
   what are they?, 53–58
   worries and obligations, 56
belief boosters
   belief-benefit reminders, 157–59
   beliefs, empowering, 104
   beliefs, power of, 107
   beliefs, removing flawed, 103–4
   beliefs, taking charge of, 105–6
   mind tools, 25–26, 153
   VisionGuidlines.pdf, 152
belief building activities.
   See also target areas for change
   "act as if" your dream is reality, 116–17
   actions, following through on, 141–42
   belief barriers, shedding, 62
   belief-benefit reminders, 157–59
   beliefs, power of, 107
   beliefs, taking charge of, 105–6
   Better Life & World Calendar, 142, 144–47
   checkups, personal-global, 150
   emotions, activating, 104–5
   empowerment tips, 149
   future generations, safeguarding, 159
   goals, educational, 49–50
   goals, global prosperity, 46
   goals and communication, 47–48
   meaning and purpose, personal, 158–59
   mental-action habits, 115–16
   mental-emotional health, 158
   progress, tracking, 143
   questions, asking high impact, 109–11
   right thing, doing the, 159
   spiritual growth, 158
   vision statement, master, 33–35
belief-energy-action dynamics
   beliefs, power of, 23–24
   beliefs and truth, 26–27
   beliefs are learned, 24–25
   beliefs as mind tools, 25–26
   director of your mind, 27–28, 149
   mind-heart distinctions, 163–65
   resistance to change, 25
Benevolink.com, 183
Bennett, Bo, 97

Better Life & World Calendar, 142, 144–47
Better World Club, 122, 181
Bhagavad Gita, 94
Bloom, Allan, 48
Books for a Better World (BBW), 136, 207
Bread for the World, 121, 175
Brown, Robert R., 46
Buddha, 163
Burke, Edmund, 173
Business Ethics.com, 177
Butler, Christine, vi

C

Cafepress.com, 177
The Calvert Group, 124, 185
Charity Flowers, 179
Children's Peace Theatre, 136, 208
Chomsky, Noam, 9
CIEE. *See* Council on International Educational Exchange (CIEE)
CIFEDHOP. *See* International Training Centre for HumanRights and Peace Teaching (CIFEDHOP)
Citizens Bank Shared Interests VISA, 146, 188
Cohen, Alan, 153
Collier, Robert, 29
communication
    act to build better, 127–31
    cultural diversity and nonviolence, 131
    intercultural cooperation, 128, 195
    intercultural understanding, 130–31, 196
    international volunteer, 129–30, 193
    judgment, 22, 27, 55, 68, 77–79, 84, 86, 199
    nonjudgment, 12–13, 78, 212
    travel to another country, 128, 193

Confucius, 15
Conscious Choice Magazine, 2
Co-op America, 178
Council on Economic Priorities, 178
Council on International Educational Exchange (CIEE), 194
Cousins, Norman, 91, 157
Cox, Rev. Sam, iv
Crescenzo, Luciano de, 95
Cross Cultural Solutions, 130, 193
Culhane, Marion, 107

D

Dell, 182
DMOZ (Directory Mozilla), 202
Domini Social Investments, 186–87
Douglas, William O., 69
Dream a Better World Day, 144
dreams. *See also* empowering beliefs; five minutes a day; personal-global dreams
    "act as if," 116–17
    action, taking, 153–54
    actual reality vs. ideal, 18
    aligning actions with, 171
    belief barriers blocking, 105
    believing in your vision, 152–53
    for a better life, 28, 109, 116
    empowering thoughts and, 115
    flawed beliefs vs., 27
    imagination and, 41
    personal vision, align with, 28, 143
    positive global change, 16
    of prosperity, 13
    vision, creating master, 31–32
    vision, defining master, 32
    vision of world desired, 120
    vision statement, drafting, 33–35
    vision statement, sample, 33
    visualization and focus, 151–52

E

Earth Day, 145
eBay, 179
Ecomall.com, 186
Edelman, Marian Wright, 133, 150, 174
Edison, Thomas, 139
education
   "conflict evolution" teaching in theatres, 136, 208
   global issues, keeping informed of, 134–35, 201
   health education in underdeveloped countries, 135
   human rights projects, 135
   illiteracy in Central America, 136, 207
   multicultural awareness, international, 137, 208
   women's education and child malnutrition, 133–34
Educators for Social Responsibility, 121, 179
Einstein, Albert, 27, 41, 163, 174
Eisler, Riane, 209
Elliot, Jane, 82
Ellis, Patricia, v
Emerson, Ralph Waldo, 154, 173
emotions. *See also* five minutes a day
   activating your, 104–5
   beliefs and, 23, 25, 65, 99, 149
   cognitive-action paradigm, 17–18
   styles of thinking, 21
   understanding, 16
empowering beliefs. *See also* belief barriers; dreams
   about, 21, 27–28, 31, 52, 55–61, 76, 116, 153
   abundance for everyone, 69
   be responsible for creating a better world, 56–57
   change and unconditional self-acceptance, 66–67
   change empowers us, 66
   choices and actions matter, 55
   cumulative impact of individual actions, 58–60
   everyone contributes to our learning, 80–81
   everyone deserves a grand life, 74
   family and community first, 79–80
   future is whatever we decide it to be, 70–73
   judgment is a statement about you, 79
   people are basically good, 85
   poverty is due to structural problems, 74–75
   power lies in making choices, 78–79
   responsibility for creating a better world, 56–57
   responsibility for things we cherish, 86–87
   self worth is given; live by sound values, 67
   treat everyone with dignity and respect, 81–82
   we are our past experiences, culture and social conditioning, 87–88
   you don't have to do everything, 61–62
Environment Canada, 190
Epictetus, 49
Everyclick website, 179

F

Facebook, 153
Fair Trade Federation (FTF), 177
faulty beliefs, 149
Federal Financial Institutions Examination Council (FFIEC), 184

Feminist Majority Foundation (FMF), 194
FFIEC. *See* Federal Financial Institutions Examination Council (FFIEC)
FINCA. *See* Foundation for International Community Assistance (FINCA)
five minutes a day. *See also* dreams; emotions
   acting on it!, 153–54
   believing it!, 152–53
   mind tools, 25–26, 153
   seeing it!, 151–52
   VisionGuidleines.pdf, 152
   visualization, 151–52
FMF. *See* Feminist Majority Foundation (FMF)
FOOD. *See* Foundation of Occupational Development (FOOD)
Food First Institute for Food and Development Policy, 121, 175
Foundation for International Community Assistance (FINCA), 176
Foundation of Occupational Development (FOOD), 180
France, Anatole, 51
Frank, Anne, 85, 119
Freedom Day, 144
freedom of choice, 22
freerice.com, 145, 154
French Proverb, 53
Friedman Lederer, Esther (Ann Landers), 81
Friends and Flags, 137, 209
FTF. *See* Fair Trade Federation (FTF)
Fuller, Buckminster, 12

G

Gaiam.com, 121, 179, 190
Gandhi, Arun, 216, iii
Gandhi, Mohandas, 74, 117, 126, 173
Gardener's Supply Company, 121, 179
George, Henry, 44
Glasow, Arnold, 113
global AIDS declaration, 153
global challenges
   abuse, physical and sexual, 4, 73, 100
   childhood death rate, 4
   child labor, 4
   climate change, 5, 230
   death penalty, 5, 12, 71, 229–30
   deaths, pregnancy-related, 4
   diseases, untreated curable, 4, 45
   drinking water, lack of safe, 4
   genital mutilation, female, 4
   HIV/AIDS, 4, 83, 153, 228, 231
   human rights abuses, 39, 74, 85
   illiteracy, 3, 50, 63, 136, 207–8, 225
   income distribution, inequitable, 3–4
   political representation, 5
   poverty, 3, 7, 14, 18–20, 35, 53–54, 58, 61, 64, 68–70, 74–76
   rape of women, 4, 73, 82, 229
   refugees, female, 4
   sexual abuse, female, 5
   sexual violence, 4
   social injustice, 13, 18, 20, 85, 97, 100
   starvation, 7, 45, 69, 75
   unemployment rates, 4
global citizen pledge, 212
Global Citizens Network, 129, 193
Global Exchange, 128, 192
Global Heroes, 195–96
global person, 7, 11–13, 212
Global SchoolNet, 137, 209
Global Volunteers, 129–30, 146, 193
Goethe, Johann Wolgang von, 154
Goldman, Emma, 89
Grameen Bank, 176
Grassroots.org, 208

gratitude and appreciation, 149
GreaterGood.com, 182
Guardian Unlimited, 205

H

Habitat for Humanity International, 129, 192
Hale, Edward Everett, 173
Hasidic saying, 161
Havner, Vance, 113
Hearth Song, 198
Heartsong Books, 134, 201
Heifer Project International Gift Catalog, 189
Heinlein, Robert, 87
Hesperian Foundation, 206–7
High Star, 13
Hillesum, Etty, 101
Hinds, Josh, 151
Hindu proverb, 98
Hitz, Randy, 134, 232
Home Exchange, 197
HREA. *See* Human Rights Education Associates (HREA)
HumaneSeal, 191
Human Rights Campaign, 146, 187
Human Rights Day, 147
Human Rights Education Associates (HREA), 202–3

I

Idealist.org, 130, 193
IFPRI. *See* International Food Policy Research Institute (IFPRI)
IFUW. *See* International Federation of University Women (IFUW)
iGive.com, 147, 183
India Shop, 180
inner awareness, 27

inspirational messages, 149
Institute of Cultural Affairs Worldwide, 205
Interfaith Day, 145
International Day for the Elimination of Racial Discrimination, 144
International Day of Cooperatives, 146
International Day of Innocent Children Victims of Aggression, 145
International Day of the World's Indigenous People, 146
International End Poverty Day, 147
International Federation of University Women (IFUW), 195
International Food Policy Research Institute (IFPRI), 133–34
International Literacy Day, 146
International Migrants Day, 147
International Mother Language Day, 144
International Peace Day, 146
International Training Centre for Human Rights and Peace Teaching (CIFEDHOP), 202
International Vegetarian Union, 122, 184
International Women's Day, 144
International Youth Day, 146
Investing From the Heart, 186
Investing With Your Values, 186

J

Jordan, David Star, 141
Jowett, Benjamin, 143
judgment, 22, 27, 55, 68, 79, 84, 86, 199
See also nonjudgment

K

Kennedy, John F., 89
Khamarov, Eli, 75
King Jr., Martin Luther, 159

Kipling, Rudyard, 95
Kiva Organization, 147, 176
Koch, Sally, 14
Kohe, J. Martin, 1
Koran, 169
Kramer, Michael, iv

L

Landers, Ann, 81
Land's End, 121, 179, 182
Leider, Dick, 35
Lipton, Bruce, 100, 218

M

MADRE, 195
Mandat International (MI), 128, 195
Mandela, Nelson, 63, 137, 209
Marshall, Peter, 61
May, Rollo, 127
Mead, Margaret, 83
mental-emotional health, 19, 158
Message Products, 187
Meyerson, Abraham, 3
MI. *See* Mandat International (MI)
mind
    content of, 16, 19, 24, 66, 70, 150, 163
    emotions, activating, 104
    empowering beliefs, 116, 153
    heart distinctions, 163–67
    history of conditioning, 88
    limitations, transcending, 111
    mental-action habits, 115
    new beliefs and thoughts, 152, 171, 203, 205
    nourishing the, 149
    observing the, 149
    open to differences, 47
    past conditioning of, 164
    power of, 95
    reservoir of beliefs, 101, 104
    tools, 25–27, 99, 153
    traps, 13
mindsets, 65, 73
mind's eye, 41, 152
mindstorm, 106
Mitchell, Connie, iii
ModestNeeds.Org, 126, 176–77
Moller, Kirsten, vi
motivational messages, 149
Multinational Monitor, 178

N

The Nation, 204
National Center for Science Education, 121, 179
Nation Books, 135, 201
Natural Investments LLC (NI), 124, 186
Nature Conservancy Adopt-An-Acre, 180
ND. *See* New Dimensions World Broadcasting Network (ND)
New Dimensions World Broadcasting Network (ND), 204
Newman, Cardinal John Henry, 100
New Society Publishers, 134, 201
Nin, Anais, 57, 174
nonjudgment, 12–13, 78, 212. *See also* judgment
Nordstrom, 182
Nouwen, Henri, 45

O

O'Dea, James, iii
OfficeMax, 182
OneCause.com, 183
Oxfam Canada, 146, 187

P

Papipaul Organization, 204
Patanjali, 111
Pax World's Funds, 124, 185
Pax World Women's Equity Fund, 123, 185
Peace Pilgrim, 39
personal-global change dynamics.
   See also target areas for change
  beliefs and quality of life, personal, 21–22
  change by education and influence, 18
  change with contents of the mind, 19
  cognitive-action paradigm, 15–18
  empowerment and prosperity, 7
  focus on the present, 19
  global citizen, becoming, 11–12
  global citizen characteristics, 12–13
  goals, personal and world community, 20
  making a difference, 13–14, 16
  purpose, three-fold, 17
  purpose and meaning, 158–59
  socially responsible change, 18–20
  vision of desired outcomes, 20
personal-global dreams.
   See also dreams
  act as if, 116–17
  checkups, 150
  checkups, scheduling regular, 150
  education goal, 48–50
  global citizen pledge, 212
  global person, 7, 11–13, 212
  goal, communication, 46–48
  goals, global prosperity, 46
  prosperity, actions for, 175–90
  prosperity goal, 44–46
  refining and focusing your, 43–44
  vision, creating master, 31–32
  vision, what is your, 32
  vision statement, drafting your, 33–35, 150
  vision statement, sample, 33
personal-global empowerment, 7, 211
personal-global prosperity
  ecofriendly travel and environmental clean-up, 122, 180
  e-mail and letter writing campaigns, 120–21, 175
  gifts to empower people and protect planet, 125–26
  save the earth and improve health, 122
  shopping and humanitarian organizations, 121–22, 177–79
  socially responsible investments (SRIs), 123–24
  spare time and, 119–20
personal well-being, 158
Peters, Thomas J., 155
Physicians for Social Responsibility, 121, 179
Piercy, Marge, 131
Pike, Albert, 159
Positive Beliefs Day, 144
Positive Futures Network, 205
Post, Laurens van der, 26
Practical Action (PA), 126, 179
prosperity. *See also* abundance
  chance and fate belief, 66
  disinformation and beliefs, 65–67
  everyone deserves, 96–97
  foreign aid belief, 68
  global goals, 46
  lack of confidence belief, 66–67
  the past is the future belief, 70–73
  people get what they deserve belief, 73–74
  personal belief barriers, 66–76
  poverty belief, 68–69, 74–75
  scarcity belief, 67–68

self-interest, fallacy of, 63–65
self-worth belief, 67
spare time and, 119–20
vision of, maintaining, 149
Proverb, 56

R

Radcliffe, Ann, 173
Ramesh, Yogi, vii
Red Hat Society, 200
resource directory
  Action Without Borders, 130
  alternative media to expand you mind, 203–5
  ambassador of goodwill, 199
  Amnesty International's Human Rights Education Newsletter, 135, 203
  animal testing and household products, 191
  banks, comparing, 184
  children, educate for 21st century, 209
  children, teaching cultural diversity and nonviolence, 199
  children, teaching respect and cooperation, 198
  choices for a better life, community and world, 171
  "conflict evolution" teaching in theatres, 136, 208
  country, taking a reality tour to another, 128, 192
  cultural diversity and nonviolence, 131
  cultural exchange, 127, 194, 224
  cultural tours, 197
  developing countries, struggling families in, 75, 189
  diversity, celebrate, 198
  ecofriendly travel and environmental clean-up, 122, 181
  ecology course, 206
  educational discussion group, 207–8
  e-mail and letter writing campaigns, 120–21, 175
  global citizen pledge, 212
  global heroes, 195–96
  global issues, keeping informed about, 134, 201, 203, 209
  global suffering and helping others, 209
  health charities supporting alternative methods, 191
  health education in underdeveloped countries, 135, 206–7
  home exchange, 197
  human rights and long-distance calls, 144, 188
  human rights and peace, 202
  human rights education, 202
  human rights education professionals, 203
  human rights groups and checks, 187
  human rights organizations, on-line, 202
  human rights organizations and credit cards, 146, 187–88
  illiteracy in Central America, 135, 207
  intercultural cooperation and dialogue, 128, 195
  Kyoto Agreement support, 181
  medicinal plants projects, 181
  mico-entrepreneurs, supporting, 187
  micro lending organizations, 147, 176
  multicultural awareness with inter national teams, 137, 208–9
  Native American communities, gifts for, 189
  on-line shopping, 182
  on-line shopping and donations, 183
  on-line shopping and fund raising, 182

personal-global empowerment and prosperity, 211
personal-global prosperity, actions for, 175–90
quotes to motivate and prompt action, 173–74
save the earth and improve health, 122, 183–84
school fund-raising, 183
shop for a cause, 182
shopping and charity support, 147, 183, 188
shopping and humanitarian organizations, 121–22, 177–79
social change forum, 205
social development and buying Indian products, 180
socially responsible investments, 123–24, 184–86
toxic cleaning products, alternatives to, 58, 190
toxic pesticides, alternatives to, 190
vacations for intercultural understanding, 130–31, 196
values, speaking out about, 199
volunteer for a global service trip, 129–30, 192
volunteer organizations, international, 130, 193
women's forum, on-line, 144, 194–95, 200
respect for others, 16, 22, 45–47, 49, 78, 81–82, 171
Robbins, Anthony, 73, 100
Roddick, Anita, 174
Roethke, Theodore, 109
Roosevelt, Eleanor, 111, 113, 173

S

Safer Cleaning Products, 190
Saionji, Masami, 47
Sandburg, Carl, 31
Sapp, Jeff, vi
scarcity, 21, 67–69. *See also* abundance
Schnitzler, Arthur, 23
Schumacher College, 206
Schwartz, David J., 51
Schweitzer, Albert, 159
Seattle, Chief, 98
self-worth, 67, 154
SERRV International (SI), 145, 178
SERVAS International, 131, 146, 196
Seva Foundation, 189
Shaw, George Bernard, 173
Shopping for a Better World, 178
SI. *See* SERRV International (SI)
Sikorsky, Igor, 103
Social Funds, 124, 186
social media networks, 153
Socrates, 154
Southern Poverty Law Center, 199
spiritual growth, 158
Squidoo, 153
Squidoo.com, 177
Starhawk, 174
Stiefel, Lester, v
Stuart, Linda, vii
Swanson, Aretta, 153
Syrus, Publilius, 79

T

target areas for change. *See also* personal-global change dynamics
discretionary time dimensions, 39–41
distractions, 38
leisure time, improving, 40–41
leisure time, making it count, 38–39

spare time and prosperity, 119–20
time choices, checklist for discretionary, 148–49
time/energy use, discretionary, 37–38
Ten Thousand Villages, 125, 147, 188
Teresa, Mother, 62
TinyUrl.com, 182, 191
Tolstoy, Count Leo, 96
Tomorrow's Children: A Blueprint for Partnership Education for the 21st Century (Eisler), 209
TomPaine.com, 205
Tracy, Brian, 105
Travel Concepts International, 197
Twitter, 153

U

Uncommon Goods, 121, 179
Utne Reader, 204

V

Vance, Juanita Louise, 31, 79, 101, 174
Van Dyke, Henry, 80
Van Hecke, Madeleine, iv
VisionGuidleines.pdf, 152
vision of prosperity, 149
visualization, 151–52

W

Where There Is No Doctor, 135, 207
Where Women Have No Doctor, 135, 207
Whitney Jr., King, 37
Winslow Green, 123, 185
Woods, John, 77
Working Assets, 188
World Association for the School as an Instrument of Peace, 202
World Day for Cultural Diversity, 145
World Day for Water, 144
World Environment Day, 145
World Health Day, 145
World Kindness Day, 147
World Refugee Day, 145
Wright, Frank Lloyd, 93
Wright Mabee, Hamilton, 60

Y

Yes! A Journal of Positive Futures, 205
Yoda, 115

Z

Zukov, Gary, 16
Zulch, Alan, vii

Author Profile

Jan L. Gault, Ph.D., is a social psychologist, university instructor, and former president of Opportunity Network West, Inc., San Francisco. Dr. Jan is the author of seven books, including *Motivational Messages for Miracle Moments; Quotes, Questions & Actions for Global Understanding; The Mighty Power of your Beliefs; Play Your Way to Prosperity*; and *Free Time: Making Your Leisure Count* (John Wiley & Sons).

Jan holds a master of science degree in educational psychology and a doctorate in social psychology. She has devoted over fifteen years to educating and empowering people to live richer and more rewarding lives. Her programs, seminars, and lectures have been presented to a wide range of audiences, and through business and professional organizations worldwide. These include the American Medical Association, National Soft Drink Bottlers Association, American Business Institute, and American Management Association.

Dr. Jan has been featured on over 200 radio/television networks and other media throughout the United States and Canada. Her articles, book excerpts, and interviews have been published in *Glamour, San Jose Mercury News, Woman, Christian Science Monitor, The San Francisco Business Journal, Bottom Line Personal,* and the *Fedco Reporter,* among others.

Jan lives in Hawaii, where she teaches university classes and has a private practice specializing in personal-global empowerment and prosperity.

Order Additional Copies of This Book and Other Books and Products by Jan Gault

Order additional copies of this book for your family and friends. Makes a great gift! Find more of Dr. Jan's inspirational & motivational books at
http://www.drjan.net/books

Download free inspirational & motivational tools at
http://www.drjan.net/bonus

Download or stream a variety of selected inspirational videos at
http://www.drjan.net/inspiration

Visit Dr. Jan's Personal-Global Empowerment Shop of Unique Gift Products

http://tinyurl.com/cgtml2

http://tinyurl.com/c27vtl

For information on training programs and consultations, please contact:

Jan Gault International©
#2701 Palani Rd.
Kailua-Kona, Hawaii 96745
Tel. 415-367-3513
E-mail: prosper@drjan.net
Web site: http://drjan.net

LET ME HEAR FROM YOU!

Warmest Aloha,
Jan

www.ingramcontent.com/pod-product-compliance
Lightning Source LLC
Chambersburg PA
CBHW031947080426
42735CB00007B/297